# How People Change
## *How Christ Changes Us by His Grace*

---

## FACILITATOR'S GUIDE

---

## Timothy S. Lane and Paul David Tripp

### David Powlison, Contributor

New
Growth
Press

WWW.NEWGROWTHPRESS.COM

CCEF

*How People Change: How Christ Changes Us by His Grace*
Facilitator's Guide

New Growth Press, Greensboro, NC 27404

Cover Design: faceoutbooks, Nate Salciccioli and Jeff Miller,
www.faceoutbooks.com
Typesetting: Lisa Parnell, lparnell.com

ISBN-13: 978-1-935273-85-1
ISBN-10: 1-935273-85-X

Printed in the United States of America

20 19 18 17 16 15 14        9 10 11 12 13

# Course Outline

# A Word of Welcome

Welcome to *How People Change*. We are gratified that you have chosen to use this course to help God's people understand what it means to be progressively transformed into the likeness of Christ. Our prayer is that *How People Change* will produce a harvest of lasting change in you and the people in your ministry or church.

*How People Change* has an ambitious goal. Our prayer is that God will use this course to change people's lives as he transforms their hearts by his grace. Our goal is that through this study, people will live more functionally Christlike lives, even in the middle of life's hardest challenges. We sincerely believe that when God cleans the inside of the dish, the outside will also become clean (Matthew 23:25). We have written this course to help people understand and participate in the grace-driven, Christ-centered work of personal transformation that God pursues in every situation and relationship of their lives.

Let us offer a few words of introduction to the course you are about to teach.

1.  Our goal is to train you and to provide you with a resource that enables you to teach people how God works growth and change in their hearts and lives, transforming them into the image of Christ. *How People Change* is intentionally Christ-centered and heart-focused. We want this material to impact you as the leader first of all; we want you to feel that it is "yours." Accordingly, we encourage you not to view it as a script you must read or memorize word for word. At the same time, we ask you not to substantially add to or alter its content. What is here has been carefully and prayerfully included and tested.

2.  Many people in our culture would call *How People Change* a self-help course because it leads people through steps of

self-examination and change. However, the Bible would use two words for this material. The first word would be *gospel*. This course is a study of what God has done in Christ to transform us from idolatry-enslaved sinners to people who are like him, zealous to do what he says is good in a world that is terribly broken. This course celebrates the truth that Jesus came to save us because we are unable to save ourselves. His work addresses the deepest and most personal issues of human experience. This course calls people to know their world, to know themselves, and to know the Lord and his grace. And it calls them to a personal commitment to a lifelong process of transformation into the image of Christ. The second word the Bible would use for this course is *discipleship*. Discipleship is walking with someone as he or she learns to walk more faithfully with the Lord. Rather than helping themselves through this course, people are being discipled by the Lord as they are discipled by you.

3.  This material should not be treated as a compilation of abstract information. This is not a theology course, but a God-ordained opportunity for you to know, confess, repent, obey, and grow. As you humbly examine yourself, looking into the mirror of God's Word and seeing your heart, your self-disclosing example will bring authenticity and enthusiasm to this material that cannot be written onto the page. Pray that God will use this course to change you and those you teach.

4.  *How People Change* systematizes God's work of heart and life transformation, but it is vital to remember that living a Christ-like life and discipling others to do so is always more than a system of change or a set of techniques. That is why this course rests not on a model or formula for change, but on the presence and power of a living, active Redeemer. Our ultimate goal is to encourage people to:
    *   Look at themselves in the mirror of God's Word.
    *   Know and rely on Christ's grace.
    *   Step out into life with renewed faith and courage.

As they do these things, they will experience the fact that they have been given "everything they need for life and godliness" (2 Peter 1:3)—all that they need not just for eternal life, but for a God-pleasing life in the here and now.

Let us say again that we are excited that you are beginning this journey. Remember that we are prepared to assist you in every way we can. Our hope is that this course will be part of a long ministry partnership between CCEF and your church and ministry.

In Christ,
Timothy S. Lane
Paul David Tripp

# Acknowledgments

It would be impossible to properly acknowledge the many people who have contributed to the content and development of this curriculum over the years. However, there are a few who must be mentioned. Thanks first to David Powlison, who developed the material that is the basis for *How People Change*. Sue Lutz edited this piece, making a much better training tool. Michael Breece did a great job of editing this 2010 reformatted curriculum. The faculty of CCEF has stood behind and supported us throughout its writing and have, in many ways, contributed to its content. Thanks to each one of you.

We want to offer a special word of appreciation to all the churches around the country that were willing to test this course. Your contribution is invaluable. You have challenged and encouraged us and helped sharpen the curriculum.

Our gratitude also goes to the churches and individuals who gave sacrificially to support this curriculum project. We could never have attempted a project as costly, as labor intensive, and as time consuming as this one without your help. You have been a constant source of encouragement to us. For all who will use this curriculum, for the churches whose ministries will benefit, and for the people who will grow and change as a result, we say thank you.

There are times in ministry when you are privileged to see God's "total involvement paradigm" ("as each part does its part") in operation. The writing of this curriculum has been one of those times.

## About CCEF

Since 1968, the Christian Counseling & Educational Foundation (CCEF) has been at the forefront of the biblical counseling movement with the mission to restore Christ to counseling and counseling to the local church. CCEF's goal is to teach people how to explore the wisdom and depth of the Bible and apply its grace-centered message to the problems of daily living. This mission is accomplished through a combination of counseling, training, publications, and conferences. These strands are tied together by a passion to equip God's people to experience Christ amid the challenges of everyday life. For more information about CCEF, go to www.ccef.org.

# Facilitator's Preparation Guide

Applying the foundational, biblical principles from this course will:

1. Help participants understand why they do the things they do
2. Bring lasting change to the lives of participants by conforming their hearts into God's likeness, right in the middle of life's challenges.

The first step in preparing yourself to teach is to review this leader's preparation guide. Be sure that you understand the material yourself and make it your own, so that you can communicate it clearly and persuasively to the people you teach.

This guide will give you an overview of the course, lesson by lesson. In each lesson, you will be directed to ten elements where preparation is critical to your teaching success. The ten critical elements in each lesson are:

1. *Homework Discussion.* Each lesson begins with a discussion of the Make It Real homework assignment from the previous lesson. Be sure that you do not gloss over or minimize this section. As participants share the ways they are being changed by the material, they experience change as a "community project." This discussion also gives you a weekly opportunity to gauge how well your students are understanding and applying what they have been taught. There will be times, as you seek to be responsive to the Spirit's work in your group, when this section is all you complete. Don't be discouraged if this happens. You are watching God do what this curriculum says he does in the lives of his people!

2. *Review.* The lessons in *How People Change* build on one another. To fully grasp the material in any lesson, participants need to understand what was taught previously. The review at the beginning of each lesson reinforces the connections in the truths that have been presented and shows how the new lesson fits into the curriculum as a whole.

3. *CPR.* Each lesson has three points of focus and application. These points are summarized at the beginning of each lesson. *C* stands for the central point that the participants need to understand and master. *P* stands for the way the central point of the lesson applies to the participant's personal life. *R* stands for the way these concepts set the agenda for the participant's *relationships* and ministry. Make sure that you understand each of the statements enough to present them clearly and simply.

4. *DVD.* Each lesson is introduced and developed by watching the DVD. The material on the DVD supplements what will be read for homework and is not just a duplication. The DVD series begins with a How People Change Leader's Introduction that is for you, the facilitator, and for anyone else who is helping to lead small groups. This session will help you to understand the content and direction of the course.

5. *Small Groups.* If you have a group larger than twelve, create small groups. These groups will remain together for the duration of the curriculum and will be the primary group in which discussion and personal sharing take place. Ideal groups for this program are between eight and ten people. Ask someone within each group to serve as a facilitator whose role is to encourage participants to share, to keep the group on task, and to watch the time.

6. *Lesson Content.* The main body of each lesson is built around key passages of Scripture, since what we are teaching about personal growth and change is defined by the Bible. These passages are not used in an out-of-context, proof-text manner. Rather, they summarize the important biblical themes on which the course is based. Encourage participants to take the time to read every passage mentioned in their study guide. Have extra Bibles available for those who may not have brought their own.

   Each Bible passage should be studied until you have understood its meaning, can apply it to the topic at hand, and can draw out the main point(s) that are critical to the principles taught in the lesson.

7. *Group Discussion.* Good teaching includes keeping the participants engaged and involved. Group discussion is one of the best ways to accomplish this. A meaningful discussion that moves beyond the "blind leading the blind" requires preparation on your part. As you prepare to teach, allow ample time for the assigned discussions. Do not omit these critical learning tools! Establish in advance your goal for each discussion, and then plan how to lead the discussion to bring participants to that goal.

8. *The Big Question.* Near the beginning of each lesson you will find "The Big Question." This question is designed to help participants take the core teaching of the lesson and use it to examine themselves, their situations, and their Lord. It is our hope that God will use these questions to further the work of transformation he has begun in each of them.

9. *Expanded CPR.* At the end of each lesson, the single statement CPR from the beginning of the lesson is expanded to three statements under each category. This is meant to be the crescendo of each lesson. These statements are simple but not simplistic. Each contains truths that are potentially heart and life transforming. Study each statement to be sure you understand its meaning and implications.

   Begin each lesson Review with a careful examination of the lesson's CPR statement, helping your students to grapple with the theological, personal, and relational implications of what they have been studying. For example, when reviewing lesson 8, begin by reading together the CPR statements for lesson 8 found before the Make It Real section. As you give attention to the CPR statements at the beginning and end of each lesson, you are bracketing the lesson content with very direct, practical, and personal application.

10. *Make It Real.* Good teaching needs to be reinforced and personally applied, or it will not take root in participants' lives. At the end of every lesson, direct your group to Make It Real. Briefly scan the section and point to one or two questions that illustrate the value in completing the assignment. Most of the homework in *How People Change* is a Personal Growth Project. Participants will be asked to pick an area of struggle in their lives and use

what they are learning to understand it and begin to change. It is our hope that, through this exercise, the course will be an actual time of personal growth, renewal, and change. The Make It Real assignments are intended to keep the course from being impersonal, theoretical, and simply the downloading of good biblical information. Instead, they give participants an opportunity to be discipled by you, and by the Lord who gives each lesson its hope.

Attention to these ten elements is critical to the success of your teaching. What follows is a lesson-by-lesson guide to prepare you to teach the principles presented in each lesson.

## LESSON 1—HERE'S WHERE GOD IS TAKING YOU

### The Big Question

- What hopes and goals give direction to your life?

### Key Scripture Passages

- 2 Peter 1:4: Participants in the divine nature
- Philippians 1:3–11: The promise of inevitable victory
- Revelation 7:9–17: A picture of our final destination

### Whole Group Instruction (total time: 80–90 mins.)

Introduction to the Course (15 mins.)
CPR
The Big Question
DVD (Show both Introduction and Session 1, 40 mins.)
Small Group Activity (20 mins.)

1. Introduce yourself to your group by stating your name, your occupation, and a brief description of your family (spouse, children), and share one of your "future orientations" when you were younger and how that determined your perspective, priorities, and actions.
2. Share with your group how you hope God will use this curriculum in your life.
3. Take time to pray together as a group.

### Homework

Read lesson 1.

Make It Real

- What dreams and expectations get you through the day and give you hope for your future? Do you ever feel hopeless? What produces that sense of despair? What were you hoping for and not getting?
- How do the things you hope and work for shape your responses to people and circumstances? When people threaten your hopes and goals, how do you react?
- Pick one place of opportunity or pressure, difficulty or blessing, where you need to view yourself as changed and carried by Christ. How will that perspective change your response to that situation?

## LESSON 2—SO, YOU'RE MARRIED TO CHRIST

### *The Big Question*

- What daily benefits are yours because of your marriage to Christ?

### *Key Scripture Passages*

- 2 Corinthians 11:1–3: Married to Christ
- Colossians 1:15–23: Christ the Bridegroom
- Colossians 1:21–23; 2:1–15: The blessings of our union with Christ
- Philippians 3:4–7: Assets and liabilities

### *Whole Group Instruction* (total time: 80–90 mins.)

Review/Discuss Homework (30 mins.)

Philippians 1:3–11 questions; Make It Real (especially question 2); reread CPR; and share which item is most relevant.

CPR

The Big Question

DVD (Session 2, 18 mins.)

Small Group Activity (30 mins.)

1. Our relationship to God is the heart of the Christian life. Describe what you think this relationship should be like.
2. What prevents Christians from having the close, intimate relationship God has made possible?

3. How do you typically think of your relationship to Jesus? As a marriage? As an employee and boss? As friends? As neighbors? As a student and teacher?

Consider the following questions on your own:

1. How is your relationship with Jesus? Is your relationship close and intimate as a bride and groom?

2. What is hindering the close relationship as God intends it to be?

## Homework

Read lesson 2.

Assets and Liabilities

Make It Real

- Have you thought about Christianity as a marriage? How is that different from the ways you have tended to view your faith?
- The core issue of 2 Corinthians 11:1–3 is spiritual purity. Where are you most tempted to commit spiritual adultery?
- What attracts you to these "lovers"?

## LESSON 3—CHANGE IS A COMMUNITY PROJECT

### The Big Question

- What daily resources are yours because you are part of the community of Christ? Are you taking advantage of these resources? What resources and gifts do you bring to the body of Christ?

### Key Scripture Passages

- Ephesians 2:14–22: Belonging to God's family
- Ephesians 3:14–21: Being loved as a family
- Titus 2:11–14: Purified as a family
- 1 Corinthians 12: Unity and diversity within the same family

### Whole Group Instruction (total time: 80–90 mins.)

Review/Discuss Homework (30 mins.)

Colossians 1:15–23 activity; Assets and Liabilities activity; How Being Married to Christ Should Change the Way We Respond to Life; Make It Real (especially question 1); reread CPR, and share which items is most relevant.

CPR

The Big Question

Opening Discussion Question (5 mins.)

> "Can anyone give an example of a time when you experienced the love of Christ through your church, small group, or Bible study? Can anyone share an example of a time when God used someone to expose, grow, or change you?"

DVD (Session 3, 26 mins.)

Small Group Activity (20 mins.)

1. Share your thoughts, feelings, concerns, or encouragements when you consider "Christians cannot grow to the fullness of God by living independently of others."

2. Who is someone you trust to reveal the truth to you?

_____

Write a question to ask this person that will allow him/her to speak honestly into your life to help you to grow and change:

_____

_____

3. Is there someone you think God wants you to confront and help in his/her Christian walk? Pray and think carefully about how to lovingly and gently approach this person.

4. Pray together as a group.

## Homework

Read lesson 3.

Make It Real

- How does your life reflect your commitment to meaningful relationships that help you grow and change?
- What opportunities for redemptive relationships are already in your life?
- If you do not have this kind of relationship in your life, what is God calling you to do so that you can participate in a redemptive community?

## Lesson 4—Life as God Sees It, Change as God Does It

### The Big Question

- How does "The Big Picture" help you to understand and respond to the grace of God as he works through the details of your life?

### Key Scripture Passages

- Jeremiah 17:5–10: The Big Picture
- 1 Corinthians 10:1–14: Life with the Redeemer in the wilderness
- 2 Corinthians 1:2–12: The example of Paul
- Psalm 1; Romans 12:1–2; Matthew 18:15–35; Galatians 5—6; James 3:13—4:12

### Whole Group Instruction (total time: 80–90 mins.)

Review/Discuss Homework (40 mins.)

Ephesians 4:4–6 questions; Ephesians 2:14–22 questions; Ephesians 3:14–21 questions; using gifts in the body; Make It Real (questions 1–3).

CPR

The Big Question

DVD (Session 4, 18 mins.)

Small Group Activity (30 mins.)

A Biblical Model for Change—1 Corinthians 10:1–14

A Biblical Model for Change—2 Corinthians 1:1–12

### Homework

Read lesson 4.

Model for Change diagram practice

Make It Real

- Identify a difficult situation or a big opportunity in your own life right now. Sort out the situation and your responses to it using the four elements of this model (HEAT-THORNS-CROSS-FRUIT). Use diagram provided.
- What aspects of the HEAT-THORNS-CROSS-FRUIT model do you tend to emphasize to the neglect of the others?

## Lesson 5—HEAT 1: The Real God in the Real World

### The Big Question

- What is your situation? What are your burdens, pressures, joys, hardships, temptations, responsibilities, opportunities, and pains—both actual and potential?

### Key Scripture Passages

- Psalm 88: God understands our deepest struggles of life in a fallen world
- James 1:1–18: Pastoral realism in the face of trial

### Whole Group Instruction (80 mins.)

Review/Discuss Homework (30 mins.)

In your small groups, go over one or two of the charts (figs. 4-4, 4-5, 4-6, 4-7) and the diagram participants created using their own personal situation. Also read Review, CPR, and the Big Question.

Opening Discussion (10 mins. whole group)

*(Leader, write responses to be seen and referred back to.)*

What are some possible ways to respond to suffering? and What assumptions do people make about suffering?

DVD (Session 5, 17 mins.)

Small Group Activity (20 mins.)

What is your response to there being a psalm like Psalm 88 in the Bible?

### Homework

Read lesson 5.

Make It Real

- Take time to think about your life. What is the HEAT in your current situation? Use the questions provided to make your responses concrete and detailed.
- Do you see any themes or patterns in your answers regarding relational struggles, responsibility, certain temptations, finances, physical suffering, and so forth? In other words, what part of the HEAT of real life tends to get to you?

# LESSON 6—HEAT 2: THE REAL YOU IN THE REAL WORLD

## The Big Question

- As God sees me respond to the HEAT in my world, what in me does he want to change? Where is God calling me to personal change right now?

## Key Scripture Passages

- Romans 8:20–22: The real world: the details
- Numbers 11:4–23: Lessons from the wilderness
- Numbers 14:1–4: Lessons from the wilderness
- Numbers 20:1–5: Lessons from the wilderness
- Deuteronomy 8:2–3: What God is doing in you in the wilderness

## Whole Group Instruction (70–80 mins.)

Review/Discuss Homework (30 mins.)

> In your small groups, discuss participant's answers to the Make It Real questions 1 and 2. Read together Review, CPR, and the Big Question.

DVD (Session 6, 15 mins.)

Small Group Activity (20 mins.)

> 1 John 1:5–10
> 1. How should we deal with our sin? How should we not deal with our sin?
> 2. What is God's response to our sin?
> 3. What then should be our response to the sins of others?
> 4. How does walking in the light lead to fellowship with God and with one another?
> 5. How can the truths of this passage encourage you in your Personal Growth Project?

## Homework

Read lesson 6.

Make It Real

- The Personal Growth Project begins in this lesson. Go over the detailed instructions with your students.

# Lesson 7—THORNS 1: What Entangles You?

## *The Big Question*

- How do I typically respond to the circumstances and relationships God has placed in my life right now? What happens as a result?

## *Key Passages*

- Ephesians 4:17—6:18: Don't live like a Gentile
- 2 Corinthians 4:7—5:10: The promise of future glory

## *Whole Group Instruction* (80–90 mins.)

Review/Discuss Homework (30 mins.)

In your small groups, share your answers to Numbers 11:4–23 and Deuteronomy 8:2–3; and Make It Real questions at the end of lesson 6.

Opening Discussion (10 mins. whole group)

*(Leader, have participants read Ephesians 4:17—6:18 and list all of the ungodly responses that Paul references.)*

DVD (Session 7, 26 mins.)

Small Group Activity (20 mins.)

- What are some reasons why God wants to bring change to our lives?
- Do you feel you can be honest about your own heart struggles with this group?
- Do you feel the Personal Growth Project you selected is the one God wants to work on in your life?
- Pray together for each other.

## *Homework*

Read lesson 7.

Make It Real

Continue Personal Growth Project using the questions in this section.

# Lesson 8—THORNS 2: Why Do You Get Entangled?

## *The Big Question*

- What has captured your heart? What cravings, desires, and beliefs rule your heart, producing ungodly reactions?

## *Key Passages*

- Deuteronomy 5:6–21: The 10 Commandments and the sin beneath the sins
- Romans 1:25: Making good things ultimate things
- James 4:1–4: The connection between idolatrous worship and ungodliness

## *Whole Group Instruction* (80–90 mins.)

Review/Discuss Homework (30 mins.)

In small groups, share your thoughts you identified in Make It Real. Identify, if possible, what FRUIT could be produced from these situations.

DVD (Session 8, 21 mins.)

Small Group Activity (30 mins.)

Read together the first part of Lesson Content, below, to the end of the list of "typical responses." Share a time when you exhibited one of these responses when something did not go the way you hoped or planned. Is there a response that tends to characterize you?

Pray together for one another.

## *Homework*

Read lesson 8.

Make It Real

- Look for places where you evidence strong emotions.
- What things tend to function as God replacements in your life?
- Reflect on the gospel from lessons 1 and 2.

# LESSON 9—CROSS 1: NEW IDENTITY AND NEW POTENTIAL

## *The Big Question*

- In what specific ways are you failing to let the CROSS shape your situations and relationships? What would change in these areas if you lived in a more CROSS-centered way?

## *Key Scripture Passage*

- Galatians 2:20: Your potential: the indwelling Christ

## *Whole Group Instruction* (70–80 mins.)

Review/Discuss Homework (30 mins.)

In your small groups, share any themes that you identified from Make It Real question 1. Share, too, which promises and truths of God's Word have been encouraging you as you identify possible idols in your heart. If you are struggling to find a theme, share one or more of the answers you wrote down and allow your small group to help you.

Opening Discussion (10 mins.)

*(Leader, ask someone to read Galatians 2:20. Ask participants to share their understanding or knowledge of this verse.)*

DVD (Session 9, 15 mins.)

Small Group Activity (20 mins.)

*(Leader, this could be done as a whole group to switch things up.)*

Share ways that you have seen God transform your own heart or others' hearts.

Pray for one another, and thank God for his transforming work in us.

## *Homework*

Read lesson 9.

Make It Real

- Where have you failed to recognize that sin's power over you has been broken?
- Where have you failed to live up to your full potential as a child of God?

- Where have you been repeatedly tempted to forget that the CROSS has fundamentally changed you?
- Where, specifically, would a CROSS-centered perspective change your relationships?
- Where is God calling you to new ways of living in the middle of the same old stuff?

## Lesson 10—CROSS 2: The Cross and Daily Living

### The Big Question

- Who are you? What is your new identity? How does believing this help you to identify and repent of the heart sins beneath your behavioral sins? How does it help you move in new directions that are pleasing to God?

### Key Scripture Passages

- 2 Corinthians 5:17: The old has gone; the new has come
- 1 John 2:1–2: Understanding your justification
- 1 John 3:1–3: Understanding your adoption
- Luke 15:11–32: Your new identity will show itself in a life of repentance.
- 2 Corinthians 7:10: Godly sorrow as opposed to worldly sorrow

### Whole Group Instruction (80–90 mins.)

Review/Discuss Homework (30 mins.)

In small groups, share your answers to Make It Real questions 1–5.

DVD (Session 10, 21 mins.)

Small Group Activity (30 mins.)

*(Leader, invite someone from the study [if possible] to lead the whole group in a time of worship. The worship time can include songs, prayers of confession and forgiveness, prayers of praise and thanksgiving, reading of Scripture, and so on.)*

### Homework

Read lesson 10.

Make It Real

- Reflect on the Bonar quote.
- Are you maintaining a biblical emphasis on Christ for you (justification/adoption) and in you (regeneration/sanctification)?

- What about Christ do you need to see and believe?
- What about Christ is more attractive than what you have settled for?
- What in Christ do you need to worship and adore?
- What Scripture passages will help you see what you need to see about Christ?

## Lesson 11—FRUIT 1: Real Heart Change

### The Big Question

- What type of heart produces good FRUIT?

### Key Scripture Passages

- Deuteronomy 6:4–6; Mark 12:28–31: The centrality of the heart in true obedience
- Jeremiah 31:31–34; Ezekiel 36:24–28: Obedience that flows from a heart transformed by the Redeemer
- 1 Samuel 16:1–13; Psalm 139:23–24; Psalm 86:11: The focus on the inward disposition—the heart
- Ephesians 3:14–21: Christ dwelling in our hearts by faith

### Whole Group Instruction (90 mins.)

Review/Discuss Homework (30 mins.)

Share with your small group how you are able to relate to Joe in the illustration from lesson 10. Share your answers to Make It Real questions 1–3.

DVD (Session 11, 30 mins.)

Small Group Activity (30 mins.)

Deuteronomy 6:4–6; Mark 12:28–31; Jeremiah 31:31–34; Ezekiel 36:24–28; 1 Samuel 16:1–13; Psalm 139:23–24; Psalm 86:11; Ephesians 3:14–21

### Homework

Read lesson 11.

Make It Real

- Take time to carefully explain the Philippians Bible Study. Review the questions with your participants.

# LESSON 12—FRUIT 2: NEW AND SURPRISING FRUIT

## The Big Question

- Where is God calling you to embrace your potential as his child and to be committed to the growth of new FRUIT that only his grace can produce? As you respond in new ways, how will your situations and relationships be changed?

## Key Scripture Passages

- Psalm 4: King David's story: In the cave and okay
- Galatians 5:13—6:10: The fruit that grows because of the Spirit's presence
- Application Passages: Matthew 18:21–35; Matthew 6:12–15; Mark 11:25; James 3:13–18; Ephesians 4:25; Galatians 5:14–15; Luke 17:1–10; Gospel of John; Romans 12:1–8

## Whole Group Instruction (90–100 mins.)

Review/Discuss Homework (30 mins.)

As a large group, discuss the Philippians Bible study.

In your small groups, share about how you evaluated your Christian life (question 1), as well as sharing your answers to the other Make It Real questions.

DVD (Session 12, 24 mins.)

Small Group Activity (30 mins.)

Bible Passages

DVD (Conclusion, 16 mins.)

## Homework

Read lesson 12.

Make It Real

- New things you have learned about life in the fallen world
- New things you have learned about your actions, reactions, and words
- New things you have learned about the thoughts, motives, treasures, idols, desires, and purposes of your heart
- New things you have learned about Christ's work, your identity as God's child, and Christ's heart-transforming grace
- New things you have learned about where God is calling you to grow and change

# Here's Where God Is Taking You

**Leader,** take time to welcome your group and acquaint them with the course using the following introduction.

## INTRODUCTION (15 mins.)

Let's become familiar with the study guide's format by briefly looking at each section. The first thing to notice is the figure titled "At a Glance: How People Change," which is on the last page of the guide, It is a summary of the *How People Change* course. We'll be referring to it often, which is why it is in a place that is easily located. This page gives you a quick preview of the model of personal change we will be learning: HEAT-THORNS-CROSS-FRUIT. The numbers in the diagram indicate the lesson that covers the topic. Next, turn to the Word of Welcome page at the beginning of your study guide. Take some time later to read this on your own. But right now turn to page iii, entitled "Course Outline." This lists each lesson that we'll cover in this course. Just like the At a Glance page, it provides a summary of the entire course. Once again, you can see that the model of personal heart and life transformation we will explore contains four elements: HEAT-THORNS-CROSS-FRUIT.

## CENTRAL POINT AND APPLICATION

Each session begins with a section entitled Central Point and Application—CPR for short. This section functions like a map for each lesson. It will give you a sense of where we're going. Notice that this section is divided into three parts. Central Point lists the core truth you need to know and remember from each lesson. Personal Application helps you to see the implications of that truth for your personal life. And Relational Application points to how each truth sets the agenda for your relationship with others for ministry.

The initials of these three points, CPR, give us a way of remembering that we are focusing on heart change. The promise of the gospel is that Christ will completely change our lives by transforming our hearts by his grace. Although we would often settle for circumstantial or behavioral change, God loves us too much to settle for that. He is intent on changing us, and because all of our actions, reactions, and responses are guided by our hearts, that is where his work of change is focused. Heart change is what bears visible fruit in our daily lives, affecting our families, church body, and communities. By changing hearts, God is changing lives—yours and those around you.

## THE BIG QUESTION

Each lesson will present you with the Big Question, which will help you take the core teaching of the lesson and use it to examine yourself, your situation, and your Lord. We hope that God will use these questions to further the work of heart transformation he has begun in you.

## LESSON CONTENT

We will spend a portion of our time viewing the DVD, which presents the main content of each lesson. Every lesson will include a time for a small group activity related to the lesson's content. Some lessons will also have an opening discussion.

**Leader,** if you are not using the DVD, spend the extra time on the opening discussion and small group activities.

## CPR

An extended version of CPR recaps the lesson and goes into more detail about its main ideas and applications.

## HOMEWORK

*1. Lesson Content:* Each week at home you should read the lesson that was previously viewed on DVD.

*2. Make It Real:* Be sure to answer the questions in the Make It Real section. This may be the most important section of your study guide because it is the place where you make the course material your own. You are strongly encouraged to do the assignments so that:

- You will know yourself and your heart better.
- You will deepen your understanding of how God transforms you, right where you live every day, from what you are to the likeness of his Son.
- You will learn how he is calling you to participate in the work of change he is daily doing in you.

One thing this section will not provide is "10 easy steps to a quick fix." Life is not like that, and we won't insult you by implying that it is! When done thoughtfully, however, these questions will help you apply the truths of the lesson to the specifics of your own life. Take time to answer them in a way that reflects where you are in your relationship to the Lord and where you believe he wants to take you. Be honest—write what you think and feel, not what you think you *should* write. Make It Real will be useful in the change process only if you are honest before the Lord. You will not be graded or judged, so treat this material like a trusted friend who can help you face a challenge. Some of your answers may be too personal to share with the group, but we hope you will share them with at least one person. Write your answers down, complete or incomplete, and trust God to help you to find him if you seek him with your questions (1 Chronicles 28:9).

At the beginning of each session, we will discuss some of your answers to the Make It Real assignment. This discussion time is important. Through it you will learn from each other, encourage one another, and allow God to use your gifts in the lives of others.

*3. Personal Growth Project:* Another way this course will encourage change in your life is the Personal Growth Project introduced in lesson 6. You will be asked to choose an area in your life where you believe God wants to change you. After prayerful thought, you might realize that God is putting his finger on your road rage, the way you play golf or talk to your children, your relationship to money, your view of your looks, your relationship with a parent or spouse, your cynicism, grumbling, gossip— or something else entirely. Next, you'll be asked to consider what it would look like for this specific area of your life—which is controlled by your heart—to undergo transformation. What is your goal, and how will you get there? As you apply the truths you learn each week, our hope is that you would begin to see substantial changes by the end of the course.

## A Word of Encouragement

Though this is a study guide with a predictable format, our prayer is that your experience with this material will be anything but predictable. We hope these lessons will instill hope and faith about what lies ahead as Christ completes his sanctifying work in you.

One of the many amazing things Christ is doing right now is changing you by the power of his Holy Spirit into someone worthy of honor in his kingdom. Someday you will receive a crown of righteousness, a crown of life, and a crown of glory from his powerful and gracious hands. "And when the Chief Shepherd appears, you will receive the unfading crown of glory" (1 Peter 5:4). "And when Christ, who is our life, is revealed, then you also will be revealed with him in glory" (Colossians 3:4).

Whether you have been a Christian for a day or a decade, we pray that the Lord will use this material to show you how your heart, mind, spirit, and will are either moving you toward God or away from him at any given moment, as well as toward or away from other people, and even yourself. There are new problems to recognize, long-standing issues to face yet again, Sabbaths to take, wars to win, lusts to lose, relationships to reconcile, and more. The calling is constant and the task enormous, but you do not undertake it without supernatural resources. As long as you live, you have hope for change. Do you believe that? "Lord, I do believe. Help my unbelief" (Mark 9:24). May the Lord bless your journey.

## At a Glance

Now let's begin our first lesson by taking a look again at the last page, the At a Glance diagram. You will see three trees under the heat of the sun. This picture represents how God changes us in the middle of the toughest challenges of life. We all have trials, pressures, temptation, and difficulty in our lives (HEAT). As sinners we all tend, in our hearts, to respond in a variety of sinful ways to what is going on in our lives (THORNS). God meets us in our sin and struggle with his heart-transforming grace (CROSS). Finally, as our hearts are transformed by that grace, we begin to respond to the same old difficulty in brand new ways (FRUIT). This is the journey we will be taking together.

Let's pray and then we will look at our Central Point and Application and the Big Question, and view our first DVD. As you view the DVDs, you can take notes in the margins of your lesson.

## CENTRAL POINT AND APPLICATION

*Central Point:* Living with God's ultimate destination in view gives hope and perspective in our daily situations and relationships.

*Personal Application:* I need to know what kind of hope directs my life. Functionally, what am I really living for?

*Relational Application:* I need to look for ways to help others live with the final destination in view.

# THE BIG QUESTION
## What hopes and goals give direction to your life?

**Leader,** begin the How People Change Seminar with the Introduction (27 mins.) and continue with Session 1 (13 mins.).

## LESSON CONTENT

**DVD** (40 mins.)

**Small Group Activity** (20 mins.)

1.  Introduce yourself to your group by stating your name, your occupation, a brief description of your family (spouse, children), and share one of your "future orientations" when you were younger and how that determined your perspective, priorities, and actions.
2.  Share with your group how you hope God will use this curriculum in your life.
3.  Take time to pray together as a group.

**Leader,** if you have more than twelve participants, divide them into small groups. The members of these groups will remain with one another for the duration of the study. Groups of eight to ten are encouraged if possible.

Explain that these will remain their groups for the whole program. Have the participants do the Small Group Activity.

## Homework

Human beings are "meaning makers." We are constantly searching for answers and seeking meaning and purpose for the events and activities in our lives: the shocking tragedy of terrorist actions, a cancer diagnosis, a friend's divorce, parenting styles, the effects of sexual abuse, racial profiling, working seventy-five hours a week, and so on. As we suffer, struggle, achieve or relax, we ask ourselves, consciously or subconsciously, *"What is the point? What's the purpose? What does it all mean?"* The answers we give ourselves—the meanings we give to our thoughts and actions—are what keep us on a certain path or move us in a radically different direction.

In little, everyday ways and in hugely significant moments, as we try to make sense of our lives, we are all crying out for some kind of change. We all instinctively know that things are not the way they were meant to be. Whether it is the fifteenth fight over breakfast between siblings who rarely treat each other with love or haunting memories of terrible abuse in your childhood, we all sense and experience that the world we live in is broken. Our days are mixed. Sure, we smile and laugh, but before the day is over we may also frown, yell, or cry.

We spend much of our time dreaming about what could be. If only the boss were more patient. If only my husband were more caring. If only my father didn't drink so much. If only my son would quit arguing and listen. If only our neighborhood was more friendly. If only we had been able to get that house. If only I could defeat my despondency. If only our church understood the single parent's plight. If only I could enjoy good health, financial stability, or the respect of friends. There is probably never a day that we don't think about change, about things being different.

As we do, we all have pictures in our mind. We look at our lives and decide where change is needed and what it should look like. The problem is that even our best definitions of change fall short. Often our desires for change aren't fundamentally wrong; they just don't run deep enough. The Bible confronts us with a hard-to-accept reality: The change most needed in our lives isn't change in our situations and relationships but in *us.*

The thing God is most intent on rescuing us from is *ourselves*. God knows that what messes up relationships and situations is people, and people are the object of his loving and lifelong work of change.

We are often at odds with our wise and loving Lord because the change he is working on is not the change we have dreamt about. We dream about change in *it*, while God is working in the midst of *it* to change *us*. What does he want to change us from and to? He wants to change us from people who "*live unto themselves*" to people who are literally *like him*. Peter says it in the most amazing way! "That . . .you may participate in the divine nature and escape the corruption in the world caused by evil desires" (2 Peter 1:4). This is real change! My selfish, sinful nature being replaced by his divine nature! God is shaping me into his own image. In the mud and muck of life, he is right beside me and his focus is me. In the middle of it all, he is radically transforming my heart by his grace, so that I am able to think, desire, act, and speak in ways consistent with who he is and what he is doing on earth. Positive personal change begins to take place when my dreams of change begin to line up with God's purposes for change. Leaving behind goals of personal comfort and self-fulfillment, I begin to reach out for Christ, desiring to be more and more like him each day. As I do this, I become more and more prepared for my ultimate destination—eternity with him.

*Here's the rub:* it doesn't come naturally to us to connect the ways we think, feel, and act in the midst of struggle with our ultimate destination of life in heaven with Christ. It is a work of the Spirit in our lives. But when we learn how to respond to that work, the impact on our lives is enormous. This is what this curriculum is about. It is meant to help you connect God's transforming grace and your future in eternity with the struggles you face every day. It is designed to help you understand how God meets you and changes your heart in the middle of the greatest joys and deepest sorrows of life.

Turn to Philippians 1:3–11. Can you pick up Paul's excitement in this passage? It is filled with reality *and* hope! Paul is clearly talking to people who need to grow, who are living in the real world with all its pressures, problems, and imperfections; yet as he thinks about them, he is brimming with confidence!

**?** *1. What is the source of this confidence?*

*Not his readers' ability to get their own act together or to make their relation-ships work or to adjust all their circumstances. Not at all! Paul's confidence is completely vertical and personal. His hope rests on a person—Jesus Christ. Paul is convinced that the good work that Jesus began in the Philippians will continue until he brings it to completion (vv. 3–5).*

Paul prays with joy when he prays for the members of this church.

**?** *2. What is he joyful about?*

*Their partnership in the gospel; Christ's continuing good work in their lives; Paul's own love for them; their sharing in God's grace with him.*

**?** *3. As you look at the passage, what does Paul want them to understand about the impact of Christ's presence on their lives?*

*All of the above, plus the fact that they can be as Paul is: positive, confident, expectant, and active.*

**?** *4. In verses 9–11, what kind of growth does Paul pray for in the Philippians?*

*Paul wants them to have a love for Christ that is:*
*• abounding in love and discernment*
*• pure and blameless*
*• filled with the fruit of righteousness.*

Paul knows something that God wants us to know too. No matter what you face today, you can be encouraged that God's good work is continuing in your life. Every step you take, God is moving you forward as you submit your heart to him. This kind of confidence and growth will change the way we respond to life. It's what moves us toward our ultimate goal—the thing for which we were made—the praise and glory of God (v. 11). Remember, Paul himself is in prison as he writes this let-ter of encouragement!

How does this passage encourage you? It's meant to encourage you to be full of hope in the midst of things you don't understand. You don't have to figure everything out. You just need to know and trust the One who does understand, and who has the power to help you. Do you look at your life as Paul looked at the Philippians' lives and his own? Or do you see things differently?

Imagine a house for sale that is a "handyman's special." One buyer sees the house as it is: the crumbling chimney, the overgrown shrubs, the broken windows, the 1930s kitchen, the missing shingles, the outdated wiring, and the roof that should have been replaced ten years ago. His shoulders sag and he walks away—too much work; not enough hope.

Another buyer sees the same house but looks ahead to what it will be when it is restored—with his kids playing soccer in the yard, guests laughing together on the wraparound porch, a wonderful meal cooking in the kitchen to be enjoyed by everyone around the table. Same house for each buyer? Yes. Same possibilities? Yes. But only one buyer who can see what he needs to do to make a new reality.

As you stand in the front yard of your life and look at the house you are living in, what do you see? What's got your eye? Do you only see the problems, give up, and walk away? Do you only see the problems and become so defensive that you angrily pretend they aren't there? Or do you see the problems the way God sees them, with hope in his power to change you?

 *5. Based on Philippians 1:3–11, what do you think God wants you to see?*

**?** *6. As you consider your own life in light of Philippians 1, how is this moment a step toward the destination God has in mind for you?*

## A Picture of Our Final Destination

For a fuller glimpse of our future, turn to Revelation 7:9–17.

This passage allows us to eavesdrop on eternity. Do you see yourself in the crowd? We are given the privilege of hearing the praises of people who suffered under the scorching heat of the sun in a fallen world. They now stand changed, purified, and free before the throne of the Lamb who is their Shepherd. This is our ultimate destination! How different our lives here can be as we learn to live with this picture in view!

Now, ask yourself this: As this multitude looks back on all that they experienced on earth, what is it that they celebrate? What in their lives has changed for the better? They don't celebrate a good job, a nice house, friendly neighbors, or financial ease. Here they are in the palace of the Lord, standing before the throne, crowned and reigning with him. There is no more hunger, no more thirst, and no more scorching heat. There is no more reason to weep. There is no more guilt to face, no more confession or restitution to be made, no more relationships to restore, no more thoughts to correct, no more justice to be sought, and no more desires gone astray. Because now their restoration is complete. The transformation of their hearts and lives has been completed, so that they are like Jesus, in true righteousness and holiness (Ephesians 4:24).

**See** also Philippians 3:20–21; Colossians 1:28–29; 1 John 3:1–3

This is where God is taking you. The final destination is his throne room where together, in white robes of righteousness and crowns on our heads, we will celebrate the one thing worth living for, the Lamb and his salvation.

Can you see yourself there? Does it encourage you as you look at your life?

## Present Promises for That Final Destination

Think again: What are you living for? What is your goal in life? Every time you raise your voice at your child or give your spouse the silent treatment, you hope to accomplish something. What is that hope? What is that goal? If you work sixty-five hours a week, you have a purpose in mind. Certain hopes and promises are directing your life. What are they?

The question is whether those hopes, plans, goals, and promises are worthy of your true calling as a child of God. Do they reflect God's purposes to renew and refine your heart and mind to make you more like Jesus? Are they in line with your final destination? And do they draw you closer to the One who will bring you there? Christianity's change process does not revolve around a *system* of redemption but around the *Person* who redeems. We focus on Christ our Redeemer—the Word of God made flesh—who gives the pattern and power for change.

## Preparing for That Final Destination

Focusing on Christ and our final destination has a major impact on our responses to problems in the present.

I can remember a conversation my wife and I had about one of our children. We were getting more filled with parental panic the longer we talked. Our fears were what we were focusing on; the things that could go wrong had captured our hearts. Things didn't turn around in the conversation—or in our hearts—until we began to help one another see the Lord, his truth, his love, his grace, and his sovereignty all clearly working in our child's life. We had to see that our hope was not in the fact that we had everything under control. Our confidence could not be that we as parents had everything tied up in a neat little bow. Rather, our confidence had to be that Christ was carrying us—and our child— through the process. We began to see that this hard moment was, in fact, a God-given step toward a wonderful destination. This prepared us to deal in a very different way with the issues that had previously produced the panic.

**?** *7. Is there someone in your life whom you look at through a lens of pessimistic fear? What might God be saying to you and your fears at this moment? How does God's perspective change the way you relate to or instruct this person?*

It is crucial not only to know your end point, but to hold it constantly before you. Life is sloppy, hard, messy, shameful, at times boring, with three steps forward and two steps back. Most often change is slow. We are tempted to believe that we are powerless to change and that all the effort is meaningless.

But the hope and good news of the gospel is that Christ has conquered sin and death, and with them every meaningless and destructive end. The Bible says that Christ gives us his "fullness" (Colossians 2:9–10). That fullness is the Holy Spirit. God himself comes to live inside us, and in him we have everything we need to be progressively transformed from what we are into Christ's own image. Because we are God's children, this "fullness" is already inside each one of us. Think about this! You have not only been forgiven, but God has come to live within you so that you will always have all you need to conquer your biggest struggles, inside and out. Spiritually, you are never really empty because you have been given the "fullness" of the Holy Spirit! That means that you can live today as if you are full. "For in Christ all the fullness of the deity lives in bodily form, and you have been given fullness in Christ, who is the head over every power and authority" (Colossians 2:9–10).

Pray that the Lord would give you eyes to see the fullness of what you have already been given. Only then can you truly change.

## CPR

### Central Point

1. Living with Christ and his body is the Christian's final, most fulfilling destination.

2. This destination adds hope to the way we see ourselves and others right now.
3. God promises to complete the transformation of our hearts into his likeness through Christ's indwelling presence and power.

## Personal Application

1. I need to acknowledge the drives and hopes that direct the course of my life.
2. I need to connect my final destination with my feelings, choices, and actions.
3. I need to acknowledge where Christ is calling me to heart change, so that being like him is my final goal.

## Relational Application

1. I need to see others in terms of the hope of their final destination.
2. I need to see the power of Christ's promise to transform their lives here and now.
3. I need to look for opportunities to help them live with their final destination in view.

## MAKE IT REAL

1. What dreams and expectations get you through the day and give you hope for your future?

- Being accepted by a certain group of people?
- A good commission, nice bonus, increased portfolio?
- Moral and obedient children, good marriage, nice friends?
- The possibility of owning the house of your dreams?
- The hope of a life of comfort and ease?
- Survival—determination to make it through this phase of your life?
- The hope of the respect and appreciation of others?

Do you ever feel hopeless? What produces that sense of despair? What were you hoping for and not getting?

2. How do the things you hope and work for shape your responses to people and circumstances? When people threaten your hopes and goals, how do you react?

3. Pick one place of opportunity or pressure, difficulty or blessing, where you need to view yourself as changed and carried by Christ. How will that perspective change your response to that situation?

4. Using one of the Bible passages from this lesson, write out a prayer asking the Spirit to help you apply what you have learned to your life and relationships.

# Lesson 2

# *So, You're Married to Christ*

## DISCUSS HOMEWORK (30 mins.)

As a whole group go over answers to questions 1–6 (Philippians 1:3–11). Then form the small groups to discuss answers to question 7 and Make It Real (especially question 2). Also while in small groups, reread CPR from lesson 1 and share which seems most relevant to you at this time.

To prepare for lesson 2, read together the Review, CPR, and the Big Question.

## REVIEW

In lesson 1, we examined what a difference it makes when we approach life with our ultimate destination in view. God is with us. He is transforming us by his grace and preparing us for an eternity with him. These three facts are meant to shape everything we do and say as we live our lives now. But do they? The answer for some of us is, "Not all the time," and for others, the answer is "Seldom."

This is where lesson 2 comes in. God doesn't just give us a call and a plan. He doesn't just call us to a right system of living. He calls us to himself, to live in a loving and lasting relationship with him that is central to the process of change. The great gift Christ gives us is himself. Only in relationship with him will we find all the good things we need.

Change, according to the Bible, is intensely personal and relational. Scripture uses the term "covenant" to describe God's willingness to bind himself in relationship with us and chooses marriage as the best way to depict this. Only when you understand what it means to be married to Christ will you understand what he has been doing for you and in you.

## Central Point and Application

*Central Point:* The hope of personal growth and change rests on my relationship with a person, Jesus Christ, who powerfully acts to change my heart and make it more and more like his.

*Personal Application:* Change takes place when I embrace the person and work of Christ in the context of my struggles.

*Relational Application:* To have an effective ministry to others, I need zeal to help them understand and experience the present benefits of knowing Christ.

# THE BIG QUESTION
### What daily benefits are yours because of your marriage to Christ?

## Lesson Content

**DVD** (18 mins.)

**Small Group Activity** (30 mins.)
1. Our relationship to God is the heart of the Christian life. Describe what you think this relationship should be like.
2. What prevents Christians from having the close, intimate relationship God has made possible?
3. How do you typically think of your relationship to Jesus? As a marriage? As an employee and boss (do what you are told and get paid for hard work or demoted for poor performance)? As friends (enjoy hanging out with Jesus)? As neighbors (stay out of each other's business and try to get along)? As a student and teacher (master what you are taught)?

Consider the following questions on your own:
1. How is your relationship with Jesus? Is your relationship close and intimate as a bride and groom?
2. What is hindering the close relationship as God intends it to be?

# Homework

## Staying Focused on Christ

As you think about the Christian life as a lifelong process of change, what things come to mind? What would you include as the key ingredients for change and growth in the Christian life? Perhaps you would mention things like personal devotions, Bible study, church attendance, reading Christian books, small group attendance, fellowship at the Lord's table, active involvement in the church, and personal evangelism. All of these things are beneficial, and all are things to which God calls us. But if these things could change us, in and of themselves, Jesus would not have needed to come. While the Christian life is not less than these things, it is much, much more. These activities are ways by which I recognize my need for Christ and learn to rely upon him. This is why these various elements have been called "means" of grace. They are God-ordained ways to commune with Christ. The Bible warns us of the danger of making these "means" "ends" in themselves, rather than pathways to a deeper relationship with Christ, and a conforming of our hearts to his will.

## Passages that Define Your Relationship to Christ

In this lesson, we will focus on three passages that help us think clearly about the living reality and practical importance of our relationship with Christ. In 2 Corinthians 11:1–3, Paul uses the metaphor of marriage to talk about being united to Christ. In Colossians 1:15–23 we catch a glimpse of Christ, the bridegroom to whom we are betrothed. In Colossians 2:1–15 we discover the life-changing benefits Christ brings us as we are united to him by faith. Let's look at these passages and see what it means to be in a life-changing relationship with Christ.

### 2 Corinthians 11:1–3, Married to Christ

Do you tend to think of Christ as a nice consolation prize? You know, if everything else in life fails you, you still have Christ to fall back on! Do you find yourself investing your time, energy, and hope in the approval of others, career success, physical health, comfortable lifestyle, and so forth, while viewing Christ as a safety net? In stark contrast, Paul presents a vision of life that makes Christ the most important and cherished thing in life. Everything *else* is a consolation prize. While Paul views these other things as blessings to be appropriately enjoyed, his concern for the Corinthians (as well as for us) is that we do not forget our relationship to Christ.

Paul is speaking with the affection of a father. He is jealous for the Corinthians' purity of heart in relation to Christ. In verse 2, Paul introduces the metaphor of marriage to describe the Christian's relationship to Christ. He speaks of Christ as a "husband" (v. 2) and them as pure virgin brides (v. 2). In verse 3, he is concerned that they will fall prey to the seduction of temptation and give their hearts to false lovers instead of Christ. Paul describes their calling as "pure and sincere devotion." In this way, Paul describes the Christian's relationship to Christ in the most intimate terms—so intimate that it is almost embarrassing! But this is what is so amazing about the gospel. God reconciles sinners to himself through Christ and welcomes us into a relationship that is intensely personal. He does not simply tolerate us; he brings us close to himself by giving *himself* to us. Christ is our husband, and we are his bride.

We are married to Christ. Consider what this means. He has made us the recipients of his affection and in turn, we are to make him the ultimate object of our affection, sharing it with nothing and no one else! This is why Paul speaks to the Corinthians as a jealous father who wants nothing to supplant or compromise this relationship. He urges them to shun the enticements of false saviors and false gospels and place their hopes and affections solely on Christ. List possible false saviors, lovers, and gospels that tempt us away from Christ.

**Leader,** have participants share their ideas during the review for this lesson. Be careful to show how often these competing lovers can be good things that become too important to us, such as career, possessions, a certain lifestyle, the respect or affection of another, power and position, appearance, physical health and strength, comfort, and pleasure.

What we see in this passage is that the most important relationship and circumstance of my life at any moment is my marriage to Christ. This foundational relationship alters the way I approach everything else. Paul's concern for the Corinthians' "sincere and pure devotion to Christ" models how my relationship with Christ should affect my agenda for my own life.

There are many models of the Christian life. Some approach it as a business, a well-planned program, or an educational pursuit. But here, Paul reminds us that the Christian life is much more intimate, personal, and comprehensive than all of these. Notice at least three profound implications of my union with Christ:

1. *If I am spiritually married to Christ, then the core of my present life is not present personal happiness but spiritual purity.* Like any other marriage, the big issue is my commitment to fidelity. Will I remain faithful to Jesus alone and not seek fulfillment elsewhere?

2. *My betrothal to Christ gives this passage a "now and then" structure.* My "now" life is preparation for my "then" marriage to Christ, when the marriage supper of the Lamb sets the stage for all eternity. Now—my life on earth—is a time of preparation for that day. The complete fulfillment of this relationship will take place in heaven, though I do experience it in part now. Because Christ is THE prize, everything else that could draw me away from him is no longer essential.

3. *For Paul, the Christian life is more than having devotions, giving money, and participating in ministry.* It is possible to do all of these things without Christ at the center of my life. For Paul, the heart of Christianity is remaining faithful to Christ in a world where many "lovers" seek my allegiance and affection. Paul's Christianity is intensely relational.

If it is true that Christ is the only prize worth living for, then he must be wonderful and amazing! Let's look at Colossians 1:15–23 to see our bridegroom.

## Colossians 1:15–23, Christ the Bridegroom

Certainly, the most important question for any prospective bride is, "Who is this person whom I am to marry?" In Colossians 1, Paul gives us a rich description of Christ our bridegroom. We encounter a stunning list of names, character qualities, and roles. Reflect on the ways each of the descriptions below should affect the way you approach life. For example, if I am married to a rich person, money will not be an object of daily concern. If I'm married to a mechanic, my cars will run well; if I'm married to a chef, I can expect to eat well. Because I am married to Christ, and this is what he is like, how should that shape the way I think about my life? Complete each of the following descriptions below in the same way:

**Leader,** there are no correct or incorrect answers here.

- Since he is God (v. 15),
  then _____
- Since he is the firstborn over all creation (v. 15),
  then _____
- Since he is the Creator of all things (v. 16),
  then _____
- Since all things were created for him (v. 16),
  then _____
- Since he is eternal ("before all things") (v. 17),
  then _____
- Since he is the Sustainer of all things (v. 17),
  then _____
- Since he is the Head of the body (v. 18),
  then _____
- Since he is the beginning and firstborn among the dead (v. 18),
  then _____
- Since he is supreme (v. 18),
  then _____
- Since he is the fullness of God (v. 19),
  then _____
- Since he is the reconciler of all things (vv. 20, 22),
  then _____
- Since he is the peacemaker (v. 20),
  then _____

What an amazing person! Who wouldn't want to be married to this groom? Here is the point: Everything I could possibly need physically or spiritually has been provided for me by Christ. In him is fullness and joy! He is my Creator, Redeemer, Sustainer . . . my true husband. It might sound strange for Christians of either gender to speak of Christ in this way. But what we must understand is that human marriage is a reflection and a type of our union with Christ, not the other way around.

If marriage is the metaphor that the Bible uses to emphasize the intimate, personal relationship I have with Christ, and Christ is the bridegroom *par excellence*, what does Christ bring to this union? Let's now look at Colossians 1:21–23 and 2:1–15 to find out.

## Colossians 1:21-23; 2:1-15,
## The Blessings of Our Union with Christ

When a couple gets married, they often start to wonder how their spouse will respond when he or she "really" gets to know them. What makes a marriage truly enjoyable is when your spouse really knows you and loves you anyway. So it is with our marriage to Christ. We cannot fully appreciate the blessings until we see ourselves as we truly are. In Colossians 1 and 2, Paul's description of Christ is set against a realistic description of who *we* are. At least these three things are true of us apart from Christ:

1.  *We are guilty of sin and alienated from God (1:21–23).* This passage says that we are sinners who are guilty and full of shame. Paul uses two powerful words to describe our position before God: We are *alienated* and *enemies* of God (1:21–23). Sin stains us and separates us from him.

2.  *We are foolish and blind (2:1–5).* One of the terrible things sin does is reduce us to fools. We are easily deceived, attracted to hollow philosophy, and enticed by fine-sounding arguments that lead us away from Christ.

3.  *We are powerless and enslaved (2:9–15).* Paul uses the best possible word to describe how trapped and helpless we are. He says that we are *dead* (v. 13). When you are dead, you are unable to do anything. You are in a condition you cannot correct or improve. Sin makes us incapable of being and doing what God intended.

Consider these facts and imagine yourself sitting alone the night before your wedding. You are filled with guilt and shame over your own foolishness, and very aware of your inability to be the spouse you need to be. What are your options? You can either run away, overwhelmed by the prospect of failure, or you can comfort yourself as you consider the character of the person you are marrying.

That is what this passage is trying to do for you. It helps you to see yourself accurately so that you will conclude that only in relationship with Christ will you find what you need, to be what you need to be. That's why, in the middle of this passage, there is a call to live in daily fellowship and friendship with Christ, to celebrate the fact that you have been granted a relationship with him by pursuing him every day (2:6–8). What Christ brings to our relationship perfectly meets the deficits we bring to the relationship as sinners.

1. *Jesus is our justifier (We are guilty and alienated).* His life, death, and resurrection free us from the guilt, penalty, shame, and alienation of sin. In 1:22, Paul says that we are holy in his sight, without blemish, and free from accusation. This is truly amazing!
2. *Jesus is our wisdom (We are foolish and blind).* In him are hidden all the treasures of wisdom and knowledge. He frees us from captivity to our own foolishness.
3. *Jesus is our power (We are powerless and enslaved).* In him we are made alive and given a new ability to live as we were intended to live.

Why is it so important to review these descriptions? Because the Christian life is built on the foundation of accepting who you really are and believing who Christ truly is. Everything you do will be shaped by the degree to which you believe and act upon the blessings that are yours in Christ.

Let's look at how this works. If you are carrying around guilt, you will tend to hide, excuse, blame, rationalize, and cover up your shame, rather than enjoy the freedom of confession and the joy of forgiveness. If you are forgetting your foolishness, you will be susceptible to pat answers, quick solutions, human formulas, and surface techniques that never truly solve problems, instead of enjoying the lasting fruit that comes from following the wisdom of Christ. If you forget your weakness, you will reduce the Christian life to a simplistic list of rules and behaviors, while being blind to the serious gaps in your own relationship to Christ.

### Illustration

Imagine a boy born into a very poor family. He spends most of his life malnourished. He is the object of scorn among his friends. He is seldom clean or properly dressed. He has little education and very few prospects for the future. He leaves home and gets odd jobs, one of them as a caddy at a prestigious country club. While working one day, he meets a young woman from an extremely wealthy family. Much to his surprise, one day she asks him to be her caddy. This begins a long relationship that, amazingly, culminates in their marriage. In an instant, his life is changed. He is the recipient of new status, wealth, power, and prestige—none of it because of what he has done or deserved. It is the result of the new relationship. His marriage changes who he is, what he has, how he experiences life, and how he will live the rest of his life. What changed him was his marriage; so it is when the Christian is wed to Christ!

As you and I come to Christ, the change that takes place is much more than change in our circumstances, relationships, or status. We become different at the deepest spiritual level. Our inner spiritual natures are transformed by the power of Christ's grace. We were once dead, and now we are alive. Our hearts were once totally enslaved to sin and now they have been freed. Our hearts were once hard as stone, but now they are soft and pliable. The changes that are the result of our union with Christ are so fundamental that the Bible says that in him we become "new creatures" (2 Corinthians 5:17)!

At the most foundational level, this change is not simply the product of good theology and disciplined obedience. Every bit of change that takes place in us is the result of our relationship to Christ. Because I am united to him, I am a new creature who is being renewed daily by his Spirit. Because I am united to him, the power of sin has been broken, and its presence in my heart is being progressively eradicated. This is what the Christian life is about. With joy I affirm that I am a new creature in Christ, and with humility I confess that there is still sin in my heart, so that I need God's grace today as much as I did when I first believed. I commit myself daily to participate in the ongoing work of heart change that is God's loving focus. Thankfully, I am *in* him; however, I am not yet completely *like* him. The Savior who made me new calls me to be committed to his daily work of renewal, which takes place in the midst of my circumstances and relationships.

### Assets and Liabilities

How do you react to the glorious imbalance of this marriage? How does it affect your assessment of what you bring to your relationship with Christ? Normally in a relationship, we assume that each person brings some strengths and gifts, but it's not true in this case. Human "assets" deceive us into thinking that we are okay when really we are people in desperate need of help.

Turn to figure 2-1 and consider Paul's example in Philippians 3:4–7. Notice some of the things he listed as the assets and strengths he thought he had. But when he met Christ, how did his evaluation of these things change? *(Read 3:7–9)*. Why did they change? Was Paul happy or sad about it? Why?

Use Paul's example as a guide to do the same kind of asset assessment for yourself on the second section of figure 2-1. What strengths, gifts, and assets do you bring to your relationship with Christ? In what ways are they liabilities in your salvation and in the process of change that makes you more like Christ? How do you respond to that? Why do you think God wants you to understand this?

Finally, complete the chart by listing what Christ brings to your relationship with him. As you can see, there are no liabilities! Why do you think God wants you to understand this? How does this encourage you as a new creature in the process of becoming more like Christ?

Everything that Christ provides changes our perspective on the things life brings our way. We no longer try to cope with life on our own, with our own resources. Knowing Christ and being found in him changes the way we experience everything! For example, how will the truth of being married to Christ change the way you respond to:

- Loss of a job
- Working at a dead-end job

- Your burden as a single parent
- The death of a ministry dream
- The injury, disease, or death of a loved one
- Chronic illness
- A difficult marriage
- A friend's betrayal
- Financial difficulty
- Chronic loneliness
- Career advancement
- Financial blessing
- A wonderful marriage
- Obedient and well-mannered children
- Perfect health

All of these things take on new significance when we realize that we experience them within our relationship with Jesus Christ.

**Leader,** a discussion guide on this material is included as appendix 1, "How Being Married to Christ Should Change the Way We Respond to Life."

## CPR

**Central Point**

1. The hope of personal growth and change rests on my relationship with a person, Christ, who acts on my behalf.
2. The Christian life rests on accepting who I really am (past and present) and who Christ truly is.
3. The Bible calls us to approach life aware of who Christ is and what he has given us.

**Personal Application**

1. I must not let my relationships and circumstances overshadow the reality of my marriage to Christ.
2. I must remember who I really am (past and present) and actively embrace who Christ truly is.
3. I must continually ask myself, "Where do I fail to appreciate what I have been given in Christ?"

**Figure 2-1.** Married to Christ: Assets and Liabilities

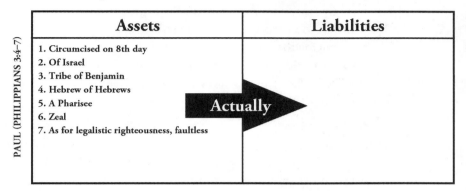

| PAUL (PHILIPPIANS 3:4–7) | Assets | Liabilities |
|---|---|---|
| | 1. Circumcised on 8th day<br>2. Of Israel<br>3. Tribe of Benjamin<br>4. Hebrew of Hebrews<br>5. A Pharisee<br>6. Zeal<br>7. As for legalistic righteousness, faultless | *Actually* → |

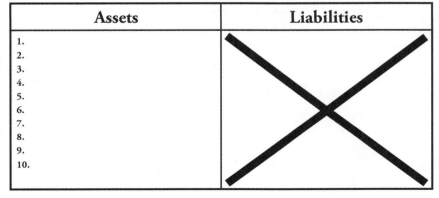

| WHAT I BRING TO THE MARRIAGE | Assets | Liabilities |
|---|---|---|
| | 1.<br>2.<br>3.<br>4.<br>5.<br>6.<br>7.<br>8.<br>9.<br>10. | *Actually* → |

| WHAT CHRIST BRINGS | Assets | Liabilities |
|---|---|---|
| | 1.<br>2.<br>3.<br>4.<br>5.<br>6.<br>7.<br>8.<br>9.<br>10. | ✕ |

**Relational Application**

1. I want people to understand that change results when they are lovingly faithful to their heavenly bridegroom, Christ.
2. Ministry to others is more than getting them to do things; it is encouraging them to actively appreciate their union with Christ.
3. I want to help people grasp what it means daily and practically to believe who Christ is and what he has given them.

## MAKE IT REAL

1. The core issue of 2 Corinthians 11:1–3 is spiritual purity. Where are you most tempted to commit spiritual adultery? What things function as false lovers? What things make you feel beautiful? Where do you see Christ replacements in your life right now? (Examples: career, recognition, success, approval, comfort/ease, health, youth, trophy kids, pleasure, certain level of economic status, theological knowledge, and ministry success)

2. What attracts you to these "lovers"? Be specific in identifying these false lovers and in confessing your unfaithfulness to Christ.

3. Write a prayer, thanking God for his love for you in Christ. Rejoice in who he is, in his blessings, and in your relationship with him.

4. Using one of the Bible passages from this lesson, write out a prayer asking the Spirit to help you apply what you have learned to your life and relationships.

# Change Is a Community Project

## REVIEW/DISCUSS HOMEWORK (30 mins.)

As a whole group, discuss answers to the Colossians 1:15–23 activity, the Assets and Liabilities activity, and how being married to Christ should change the way we respond to life.

In small groups, discuss Make It Real (especially question 1); reread CPR, and share which item God is impressing upon their hearts currently.

Next, read together CPR and the Big Question for lesson 3.

## CENTRAL POINT AND APPLICATION

*Central Point:* God's work of personal transformation is intended to take place within the community of God's people.

*Personal Application:* I need to be committed to a lifestyle of mutually helpful relationships.

*Relational Application:* I want to help others pursue relationships that promote biblical growth and change.

## THE BIG QUESTION

What daily resources are yours because you are part of the community of Christ? Are you taking advantage of these resources? What resources and gifts do you bring to the body of Christ?

## Lesson Content

### Opening Discussion (5 mins.)

**Leader,** this discussion could take place as a whole group or while they are sharing in their small groups:

Ask, "Can anyone give an example of a time when you experienced the love of Christ through your church, small group, or Bible study?"

"Can anyone share an example of a time when God used someone to expose, grow, or change you?"

### DVD (26 mins.)

### Small Group Activity (20 mins.)

1. Share your thoughts, feelings, concerns, or encouragements when you consider "Christians cannot grow to the fullness of God by living independently of others."
2. Who is someone you trust to reveal the truth to you?

   _____

   Write a question to ask this person that will allow him/her to speak honestly into your life to help you to grow and change:

   _____

   _____

   _____

3. Is there someone you think God wants you to confront and help in his/her Christian walk? Pray and think carefully about how to lovingly and gently approach this person.
4. Pray together as a group.

## Homework

Have you ever heard someone say, "You've made your bed; now lie in it"? As Christians, we know that nothing could be further from the gospel. Can you hear the two main lies in this statement?

1. "The problems you've created are irreversible, so you are stuck in your own mess."
2. Not only are you stuck forever, you are totally on your own."

In other words, don't expect help from anybody. If things are going to change, you'd better find a way to fix them yourself—and don't try to join the rest of us (who have no problems) until you do.

When Christ brings us into the family of God, no matter how much we have messed up, we are never alone again. Yet many believers latch onto the hope of personal change while clinging to the individualism of our society. They have a "Jesus and me" mentality as they battle sin and seek to become more like Christ. At first we might think, *Why not? After all, getting involved with people is complicated and time consuming. Who needs it? It's not very efficient when we have a lot of personal changing to do.*

But God has a bigger—and, frankly, messier—plan. Change is something God intends his people to experience *together*. It's a corporate goal. What God does in each of us as individuals is part of a larger story of redemption that involves all God's people through the ages. You are part of the story and part of the family already, and that is the context in which personal change takes place in your life. That is also what we hope you will experience in this course. Change within community is counterintuitive to the way we often think, but Scripture clearly presents it as God's way of making us more like Christ.

## God Himself Lives in Community

Have you ever wondered why? The most important reason is often overlooked: *God himself is a community!* The Father, the Son, and the Holy Spirit live together in perfect fellowship, harmony, and unity. What each person of the Trinity is and does is always in union with the others. That even includes our salvation! At great personal cost, God the Father, Son, and Holy Spirit all played a part in bringing us into the family of God. Their perfect fellowship as the Trinity was disrupted so that we could be brought into fellowship with God.

Look at the way Scripture talks about this in Ephesians 4:4–6. Did you notice that Paul uses the word *one* seven times? The unity of God is meant to lead to unity in his family.

*1. What unity do we share as believers?*

*One body, one hope, one faith, one baptism, one God who is over all and through all and in all.*

The message is clear: God is a community and this is stamped onto all he creates.

## Belonging to God's Family

When the apostle Paul was discipling new believers, he repeatedly reminded them there was help in Christ *and* in Christ's people, the church, in good times and bad. Let's look at two specific passages where Paul encourages the Christians at Ephesus to think of themselves as part of something new—something bigger. Read Ephesians 2:14–22.

 *2. In this passage, what is God seeking to produce in us, his people?*

*God is producing one new body, people who are joined together and moving toward one another; he is producing a dwelling place for his Spirit.*

 *3. What has God done to make this possible?*

*Jesus died on the cross to abolish the dividing wall and make this possible—it must be very important to him.*

It is impossible to read this passage and come away with the idea that Christianity is a "just-me-and-God" religion. Have you ever heard someone say, "Yes, I am a Christian, but I don't go to church. Why do I need that when I have the Lord?" This passage makes it clear that our salvation is something that connects us to God *and* his people. It's not just in heaven that we will be united around the throne of God. Our personal relationship with God links us to other believers *now*.

Notice how Paul brings this out. He says that God has "destroyed the barrier" "to create in himself one new man." We are "fellow citizens with God's people and members of God's household." We are "being built together to become a dwelling place in which God lives." We can't become the Christians we are meant to be by being alone with God. That is not God's purpose. What we become, we become together.

*4. How does this vision impact you? Does it surprise you? Intimidate you? Annoy you? Encourage you? How much does your life currently allow you to develop relationships that are deep enough to help you grow and change? What are some of the obstacles to such relationships?*

American culture may idolize the Lone Ranger, Clint Eastwood, and Superman as heroes who right wrongs and ride out of town alone, but that solitary approach to change is foreign to Scripture. When we are accepted by God through faith in Christ, we are adopted into his family and made members of his body (Ephesians 5:29–30). This is not necessarily the simpler way; being involved with people is inefficient, complicated, and time consuming. There are so many more ways for things to go wrong! But these are some of the very reasons why community is such a big part of God's plan to transform us into the image of Christ. The more we understand our own hearts, the more we see that it takes a work of God's grace to transform self-absorbed individuals into a community of love. Being in community shows us our need for change *and* helps bring it about!

## Being Loved as a Family
Read Ephesians 3:14–21.

*5. What is Paul praying for in this passage?*

He wants the Ephesian believers to have strength to grasp the nature of God's love. It is tempting to see this as a prayer for individuals to truly know God and understand his love, but this knowledge and "power through his Spirit" comes to us as we are part of a community.

*6. What language does Paul use that shows he believed these things would come from God through community?*

*Again, look at the language Paul uses. Do you get a sense of how big the love of Christ is? Can you imagine what it would take to really tap into it? The love of Christ is so long and high and deep (infinite, in other words!) that we cannot see this love or experience it all by our finite selves. We have to grasp it "together with all the saints" (v. 18), much like a jury relies on twelve different minds to come to a full understanding of the truth.*

*Paul's prayer that they would, together, be rooted and established in love is the only way they can be filled with the fullness and power of God. As isolated individuals, they cannot reach the level of maturity God has designed for them. This fullness happens as they live in a loving, redemptive community with one another.*

When we look ahead to Ephesians 4, we see that Paul follows his prayer with all sorts of practical instructions on how to pursue and preserve the unity of this community. These are some of the ways our personal transformation is worked out within the family of God.

If, as we see in 4:4–6, God himself lives in community, could we really expect him to want anything different for us? If his redemptive purposes caused him to enter our world and get close to us, should we be surprised that he calls his children to do the same with each other? The things we need to do to enjoy deep love and fellowship with God and each other are the very things that make us less self-centered and more like Christ. It *is* the change he is after!

## Purified as a Family

We have seen that understanding God's love as God's people brings us to maturity or "fills us to all the fullness of God." Another component of Christian growth involves saying no to what is harmful and yes to the things that produce life and godliness.

Read Titus 2:11–14. This is another passage that first appears to present God's grace to individuals, who then are commanded to use God's grace as a way to privately clean up their act. However, as the passage describes the final goal of God's grace, it says that Jesus gave himself to us "to purify for himself a *people* . . . eager to do what is good" (v. 14). The ultimate goal of God's grace is to produce an active, healthy, unified body of believers. It's a full-fledged family freed from sin and its enslaving ways. It is this people, purified and zealous for good works, who are God's precious inheritance.

Just as in Ephesians, this chapter is followed by instructions for corporate Christian living. We need each other's help as we learn to say yes and no to the right things! Paul calls believers to live in a way that helps people to be built up as well as built together, and he adamantly warns against divisiveness.

Divisiveness conjures up images of one person or group intentionally leading others away from the whole, leaving the rest of the body to suffer. It *is* damaging when people quarrel and leave, but the body of Christ is also deformed and disabled when people never fully join it in the first place.

Paul describes this vividly in 1 Corinthians 12, where he talks about the family of believers as a physical body. Read 1 Corinthians 12:12. Each believer receives gifts from the Holy Spirit to be used "for the common good" (v. 7). We are to live as unique and vital parts of Christ's body, connected to serve and be served by the rest of the body (vv. 12, 14). No one part should think of itself as useless, especially when compared to more prominent or "glamorous" parts (vv. 15–27). Think about the gifts God has given you.

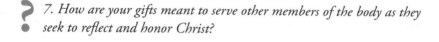 7. *How are your gifts meant to serve other members of the body as they seek to reflect and honor Christ?*

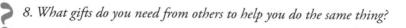 8. *What gifts do you need from others to help you do the same thing?*

Think of what happens in a church when there is a death in a family. The pastor and others seek to comfort the family with the promises of Scripture. Other people bring meals, watch the children, make phone calls, run errands, clean the house, drive the grieving survivors to the funeral home, and help them make arrangements. Still others help them with banking, budget, and insurance matters. Others just come to weep with those who mourn. How many of you have experienced the love of Christ in this multiplicity of ways? Wouldn't you agree that all the different elements combined together more fully reveal the love and power of God? Doesn't it provide more hope for the future, more encouragement to trust the Lord, more strength to do and be what God calls us to be? Everything is more powerful when it is combined with the ministries of the rest of the body.

What is the point of all this? God's work of change has relationships both as a necessary means and a wonderful goal. Humble community is not the icing on the cake of Christianity. In a real way, it *is* the cake. These relationships of love are a means of personal growth, a mark of God's people being purified, and a clear argument to the world for the truth of the gospel.

## CPR

**Central Point**

1. A Christian is not only a child of God, but a member of the family of God.
2. Christians cannot grow to the fullness of God by living independently of others.
3. Personal transformation takes place in the context of redemptive community.

**Personal Application**

1. I continually need to learn more about God's love for me in Christ, and I cannot do this alone.
2. I need to understand my gifts and my role in the larger body of Christ.
3. God calls me to be committed to a lifestyle of mutually edifying relationships.

**Relational Application**

1. I want to pray for others to gain a greater understanding of God's love for them in Christ.
2. I want to help others understand and own their vital place in the body of Christ.
3. I want to help others grasp the privilege and responsibility of participating in intimate Christian relationships that promote biblical growth and change.

## MAKE IT REAL

1. How does your life reflect your commitment to meaningful relationships that help you grow and change? What things get in the way or serve as replacements for you? Here are some possibilities:

- The busyness of life (keeping relationships distant and casual)
- Being totally immersed in friendships that are activity- and happiness-based
- Conscious avoidance of close relationships (too scary or messy)
- Formal commitment to church meetings and activities but no real connections to people
- One-way, ministry-driven relationships (always ministering to others but never allowing yourself to be ministered to)
- Self-centered, self-absorbed, "meet-my-felt-needs" relationships that keep you always receiving but seldom giving
- A private, "just-me-and-God" approach to the Christian life
- Theology as a replacement for community—knowing God as a life of study, rather than the pursuit of God and his people

2. What opportunities for redemptive relationships are already in your life? (marriage, friendship, parents, small group, extended family, ministry partner, etc.) Are you committed to and experiencing the personal transformation that God has planned for these relationships? If not, what things are in the way?

3. If you do not have this kind of relationship in your life, what is God calling you to do so that you can participate in a redemptive community? Are there new relationships that need to be made? Present relationships that need to be strengthened or restructured? Relationships that need to be restored?

4. Using one of the Bible passages from this lesson, write out a prayer asking the Spirit to help you apply what you have learned to your life and relationships.

# Lesson 4

# *Life as God Sees It, Change as God Does It*

## <u>Review/Discuss Homework</u> (40 mins.)

As a whole group, discuss questions 1–6 in the Lesson Content section for lesson 3. In small groups, discuss questions 7 and 8 from Lesson Content and questions 1–3 from Make It Real.

Read Review, CPR, and the Big Question below.

## <u>Review</u>

Let's review where we have been so far. In lesson 1, we learned that there is a valid reason to *hope for change*. Real change is not only possible but actually happening because Christ, in all of his power, changes us fundamentally at the moment we first trust in him. I am a new creation in Christ, and I will enjoy nothing less than total transformation in the future! This wonderful vantage point begins in the past with my conversion and culminates in the future with my glorification. It gives me a deep hope and confidence as I struggle and grow in the present. In lesson 2, we considered the Redeemer, Jesus Christ, the *person who changes us*. He provides not only the resources for change but himself as well. This relationship supernaturally transforms our hearts. In lesson 3, we learned that God has provided a wonderful *context for change*. God knows that we cannot do this alone; we need one another. God has placed us in the middle of a ministering community where daily help is available. With this foundation, we can begin to examine the *process of change* in lessons 4–12. This lesson will introduce the various elements that are a part of the change process.

## CENTRAL POINT AND APPLICATION

*Central Point:* Practical hope, comfort, and direction result from looking at our lives and our world from God's big picture perspective.

*Personal Application:* I always need to evaluate myself in light of what God says about himself, me, my world, and change.

*Relational Application:* I need to help people see the hope found in looking at their lives from God's big picture perspective.

# THE BIG QUESTION

How does "The Big Picture" help you to understand and respond to the God of grace as he works through the details of your life?

## LESSON CONTENT

### DVD (18 mins.)

**Leader,** to introduce the purpose of the following activity, you might say something like, "To help us understand the idea of HEAT-THORNS-CROSS-FRUIT, we are going to do a part of the homework together in our small groups. As a small group, turn to 1 Corinthians 10:1–14 in your Bibles. Together, read the section in your study guides about how the 1 Corinthians passage reflects the HEAT-THORNS-CROSS-FRUIT model. For part of your homework, you will be filling in the diagram based on 2 Corinthians 1:1–12 and a diagram based on a current situation or opportunity."

### Small Group Activity (30 mins.)

Turn in your Bibles to 1 Corinthians 10:1–14. Move between the Scripture passage, the explanation of the passage as related to the model, and the model itself in figure 4-2.

If you have time, begin filling in figure 4-3 based on 2 Corinthians 1:1–12. What you do not finish together, complete on your own for homework.

## HOMEWORK

### The Big Picture

Do you ever feel lost in the middle of your own world? Sure, you know a lot about yourself, God, and others, but you are not sure how to put it all together. You don't know why your marriage is struggling. You don't know why you battle with depression. For the life of you, you cannot understand why your teenage son has become so adversarial. It is these experiences that this lesson and this curriculum address.

Think of it this way. If you are lost in the middle of a big city, what do you need? The tempting answer would be specific and detailed directions. But, in fact, you need more! If all you received were particular instructions to one destination, you would be lost once again after you followed them. What you really need is the helicopter overview of the whole city implanted in your brain—*the big picture*. Then you will always know where you are and where you need to go.

When you read your Bible, it doesn't always seem like it gives you a helicopter view of all of life. Scripture can seem like a haphazard collection of stories, poems, teachings, and commands. Yet when carefully examined, the Bible provides the essential elements that give an overall picture of life as God sees it and change as God does it. Only when you have an overall sense of what God is doing can you make sense of all the details of your everyday life. This lesson will introduce you to four elements that the Bible repeatedly includes in the change process God institutes in the lives of his children. Understanding how God typically uses daily life to change our hearts is an essential part of this growth and change process.

## How the Bible Gives Us the Big Picture

Although this lesson will refer to God's "big picture," we will be the first to say that the Bible does not explain the model we are introducing in one specific passage. Rather, different elements of this model are woven through many passages of Scripture. The same elements are often presented but with different language, order, and emphasis. However, once you begin to identify these elements as they occur in Scripture, they start to simplify and enrich your understanding of what the Bible teaches, resulting in practical wisdom for you. The wonderful thing about this big picture model is that it is the story of every believer's life. God has already made us a part of it and invites us to live with him inside the plot. Let's begin by looking at the elements of this Big Picture in figure 4-1.

*Figure 4-1.* How Do People Change?
Jeremiah 17:5–15

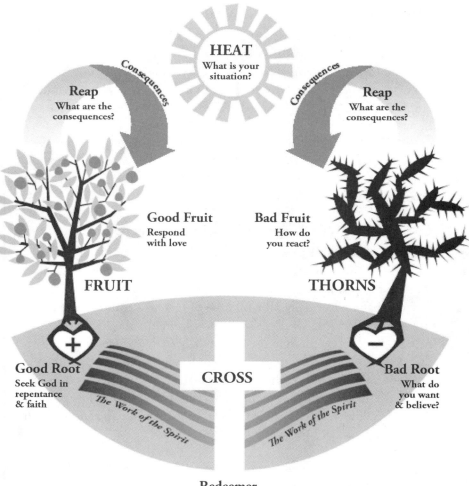

HEAT
What is your
situation?

Consequences

Reap
What are the
consequences?

Consequences

Reap
What are the
consequences?

Good Fruit
Respond
with love

Bad Fruit
How do
you react?

FRUIT

THORNS

Good Root
Seek God in
repentance
& faith

CROSS

The Work of the Spirit

The Work of the Spirit

Bad Root
What do
you want
& believe?

Redeemer
Who is God and what does
he say and do in Christ?

## HEAT (What is your situation?)

You and I are always reacting to things that are happening around us. Whether it is the scorching heat of difficulty or the unexpected rain of blessing, you are always responding to whatever is coming down on you. The Bible presents a shockingly real picture of a fallen world. It is honest about the things that happen here.

## THORNS (How do you react? What do you want and believe?)

You and I are never really passive. We are always acting, reacting, and responding to the "heat" (or "rain") in our lives. Maybe it's a tough boss or a crazy extended family. Perhaps it is a rebellious child or a chronic sickness. Maybe it's a new career opportunity or a newly acquired inheritance. Whatever it is, the Bible helps us to see how we react to the "heat," in our hearts and our outward behavior. It reminds us that sinners tend to respond to the fallen world sinfully and each reaction yields a harvest of consequences. Scripture also makes it clear that these responses are not forced on us by the pressures of the situation. Rather, they flow out of the thoughts and motives of our hearts.

## CROSS (Who is God, and what does he say and do in Christ?)

The God of the Bible presents himself as "an ever-present help in trouble." The ultimate example is Christ, who came to a fallen world to live, die, and rise again. He gave us everything we need to respond in a godly way to what we face daily. The promise of the cross is not just renewed strength or enhanced wisdom; it is a new heart that begins to evidence new strength and wisdom in the face of daily trials and blessings. Christ, the Redeemer, gives us himself and in so doing remakes us from the inside out. Each of us is in the process of being remade to reflect the character of Jesus himself. This is truly amazing! His patience, love, mercy, courage, boldness, justice, and grace can be expressed more and more in and through us as we grow into his likeness.

## FRUIT (Seek God in repentance and faith. Respond with love.)

Because of what Christ has done, we can respond to the same old pressures in a brand new way. Out of hearts renewed by him, we behave differently in response to the circumstances of life. These new responses produce a harvest of fruitful consequences in our lives and the lives of others.

Let's look at three passages where the elements of the Big Picture can be found.

### Jeremiah 17:5–10

The Bible typically uses concrete images to illustrate spiritual truths. Jeremiah 17:5–10 is a good example. Look at the main images in this passage. In verse 8, the image of Heat is used to describe life in a fallen world. In verse 6 the image of a Thorn Bush in the wasteland represents the ungodly person who turns away from the Lord. In verses 5 and 7, there is a clear reference to the Lord. He is the Redeemer who comforts, cleanses, and empowers those who humbly trust in him. We represent this part of the passage by the Cross to capture the redemptive activity of God on our behalf. In verses 7 and 8, the image of a Fruitful Tree emerges, representing the godly person who trusts in the Lord. In the midst of these images, verses 9 and 10 show us a God who does not simply focus on our behavior. Though he does not ignore behavior, his focus is on our hearts. He is the searcher of hearts because they are central in the change process he undertakes as our Redeemer.

This gives us a simple but helpful view of life that involves four basic elements described metaphorically. We have the HEAT. This is the person's situation—the real world with all of its difficulties, blessings, temptations and enticements. We have THORNS (the bush)—the person's ungodly response to the situation. This includes behavior, the heart that drives the behavior, and the consequences that follow. We have the CROSS—that is, the presence of God in all his redemptive glory and love. He brings comfort, cleansing, and power to change. Finally, we have FRUIT—the person's new, godly response to the situation as a result of God's redemptive power at work in the heart. This includes behavior, the heart renewed by grace, and the consequences that follow. Thus we have a simple biblical picture that captures the major elements of change in the midst of life: HEAT-THORNS-CROSS-FRUIT.

Now, let's look together at two passages and organize them in light of these four elements. As we do this, we will begin to see how this big picture is basic to a biblical view and understanding of all of life. All of the elements are in each passage but presented in different ways. In 1 Corinthians 10:1–14 we see the elements presented in the general context of dealing with life's hardship (the model). In 2 Corinthians 1:2–11, the same elements are presented within the context of Paul's personal experience (a case study).

## Read 1 Corinthians 10:1–14

Let's use figure 4-2 to consider this passage from the vantage point of the picture we saw in Jeremiah 17. First, we see HEAT. In verses 11–14, Paul is using the real-life experience of Israel in the wilderness to help the Corinthians understand their own situation. We should be encouraged by the Bible's honesty about what we experience in this fallen world. God understands what is going on around us and in us. We will be looking at Numbers 11—14 to understand what Paul is saying. What was Israel's situation? What pressures, temptations, blessings, challenges, and entice-ments did they face? How did it compare to the Corinthians' situation? How does it compare to ours? An overview of Numbers 11—14 is pro-vided at the end of this chapter.

Second, we see THORNS. In 1 Corinthians 10:5–10, Paul details the ungodly ways Israel responded to the heat (idolatry, pagan revelry, sexual immorality, testing the Lord, and grumbling). In verses 7b–9a and 10a he emphasizes their specific *behavior*. In 5, 9b, and 10b he mentions the *consequences*. In verses 6–7a he focuses on the *heart* out of which the behavior grows.

Third, we see the CROSS. In verses 1–4 Paul speaks of God's pres-ence and power with Israel during their time in the wilderness ("All ate the same spiritual food and drank the same spiritual drink; for they drank from the spiritual rock that accompanied them, and that rock was Christ."). How amazing that the same Christ that is now with the Cor-inthians (and with us) was with Israel! Living in reliance on him, in the midst of life's difficulties, is at the very heart of what God is seeking to produce in each of us.

Finally, we see FRUIT. In verses 11–14, Paul calls his readers to embrace Christ. Verse 11 is a reference to Jesus' first coming. Paul wants his readers to see how privileged they are to live in full view of the com-ing of the Messiah and to have full access to the blessings that are ours because of him. In verses 11–12, Paul speaks of a new *heart* that embraces Christ and engages in humble self-examination. In verses 13–14, Paul describes new *behavior* that includes new resolve to stand up under temp-tation (13) and a new watchfulness that sees the tendency to slide toward idolatry. Paul is envisioning initial as well as long-term change!

*Figure 4-2.* A Biblical Model for Change (1 Corinthians 10:1–14)

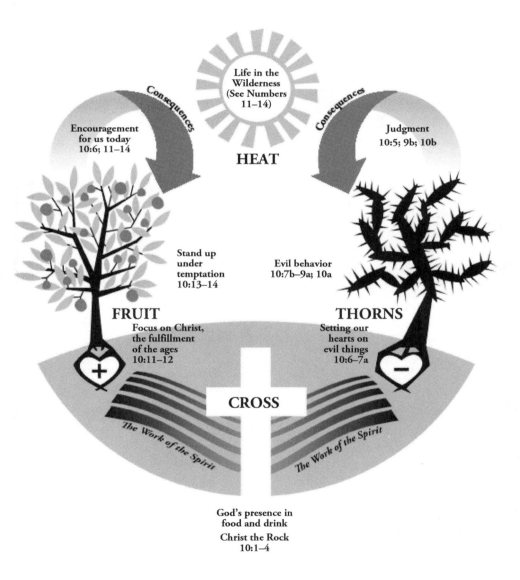

## Figure 4-3. A Biblical Model for Change (2 Corinthians 1:1–12)

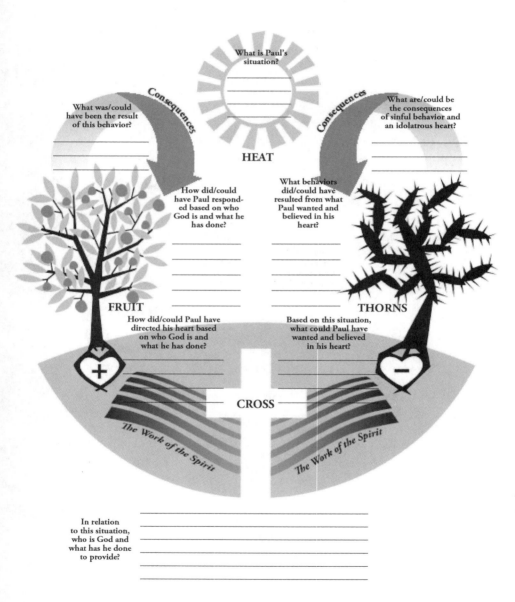

What is Paul's situation?

**Consequences**

What was/could have been the result of this behavior?

What are/could be the consequences of sinful behavior and an idolatrous heart?

**Consequences**

**HEAT**

How did/could have Paul responded based on who God is and what he has done?

What behaviors did/could have resulted from what Paul wanted and believed in his heart?

**FRUIT**

**THORNS**

How did/could Paul have directed his heart based on who God is and what he has done?

Based on this situation, what could Paul have wanted and believed in his heart?

**CROSS**

*The Work of the Spirit*

*The Work of the Spirit*

In relation to this situation, who is God and what has he done to provide?

## 2 Corinthians 1:2–12

Let's look now at 2 Corinthians 1:2–12 to watch someone actually using HEAT-THORNS-CROSS-FRUIT to reflect on his own life. To do this we have provided an illustration of the "biblical big picture" we have been examining (see fig. 4-3). In 2 Corinthians 1, Paul is looking at his own life in terms of these four elements. Use figure 4-3 to organize 2 Corinthians 1:2–12 according to the elements of HEAT-THORNS-CROSS-FRUIT.

Do you see that although these passages refer to situations taking place in different eras and circumstances, the same four elements help us to understand what is going on from God's perspective? In each case, God sees us, meets us, and changes us right in the middle of life's challenges.

Understanding the overall picture of life and change in a fallen world not only helps you understand the Bible better, it also helps you see how practically helpful the Bible can be in the process of change. In lessons 5–12, we will take a more detailed look at these four elements and their part in God's process of changing us to be more like him. This offers you a wonderful opportunity to grow in areas where you need to grow. It will also provide a foundation for you to help others.

In the lessons to come, we will look carefully at this four-part picture of how God changes us. We will also give you an opportunity to apply what you learn to your own life as you live under the "heat" every day.

Let's look at some additional passages using "The Big Picture." Select one of the passages given to complete figure 4-4. It should help you to see that this model is a biblical way to think about life and a helpful way to understand the various situations we face.

## CPR

**Central Point**

1. Practical hope, comfort, and direction result from looking at our lives and our world from God's overall perspective on change.
2. The Bible is honest about the trouble we face in a fallen world.
3. Scripture's description of the change process that God oversees in our lives can be described using the categories of HEAT, THORNS, CROSS, and FRUIT.

### *Figure 4-4.* A Biblical Model for Change

Select one of the following passages to practice applying this model:
Psalm 1; Matthew 18:15–35; Galatians 5—6; or James 3:13—4:12.
(Possible answers can be found in figs. 4-6 through 4-9.)

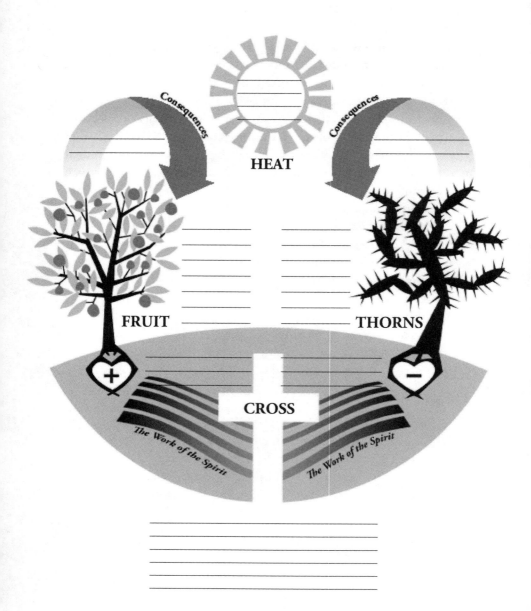

**Personal Application**

1. I always need to evaluate myself in light of what God says about me, my world, and change.
2. The Bible's honesty about life in this world invites me to be honest about my difficulties and my responses to them.
3. I need to learn how to examine myself using the simple categories God provides in his Word (HEAT, THORNS, CROSS, and FRUIT).

**Relational Application**

1. I need to help people see the hope found in looking at life from God's perspective.
2. I need to encourage people with the way the Bible accurately and honestly describes what we face every day.
3. A significant aspect of a wise and helpful ministry is to help others see themselves from the perspective of these simple biblical categories (HEAT, THORNS, CROSS, and FRUIT).

As Christians, we are not either a fruit tree or a thorn tree; instead, our lives will always contain some combination of fruit and thorns. As we turn to Christ in repentance and faith, the Spirit will enable us to grow more fruitful.

## MAKE IT REAL

1. Identify a difficult situation or a big opportunity in your own life right now. Sort out the situation and your responses to it using the four elements of this model. Your struggle might be physical suffering or the kind of suffering we experience when someone sins against us. Or your struggle could be a personal struggle with a sin pattern. As you complete figure 4-5, think about what shapes the way you see the circumstance that you are in and how you are responding to your circumstances.

2. What aspects of the HEAT-THORNS-CROSS-FRUIT model do you tend to emphasize to the neglect of the others? Some examples:

- Pharisees emphasized behavior over the heart.
- People who have suffered or been abused tend to emphasize the situation ("heat") over everything else.

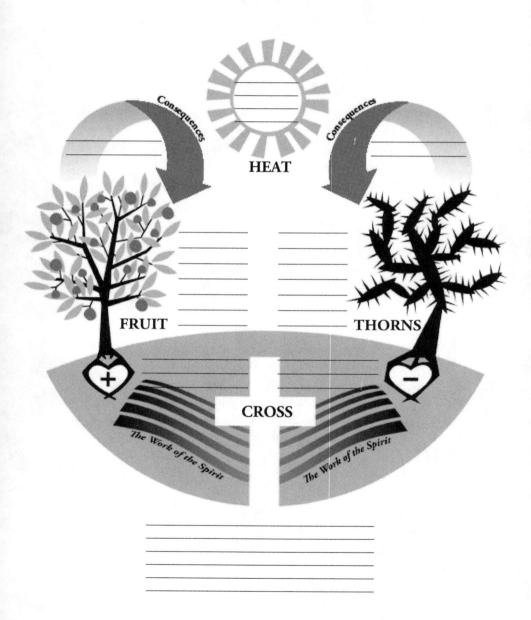

*Figure 4-5.* **A Biblical Model for Change**
For use with Make It Real question 1.

HEAT

Consequences

Consequences

FRUIT

THORNS

CROSS

The Work of the Spirit

The Work of the Spirit

- The overly introspective person tends to spend his time in endless heart examination.
- The "Jesus-and-me" person tends to focus on the cross in isolation from everything else.
- The legalist tends to look only at consequences and conclude that bad consequences prove that there must have been bad behavior (see Job's counselors).

3. Using one of the Bible passages from this lesson, write out a prayer asking the Spirit to help you apply what you have learned to your life and relationships.

*Figure 4-6.* The Voices and Images of Misleading Counsel Influence Us (Psalm 1, Romans 12:1–2).

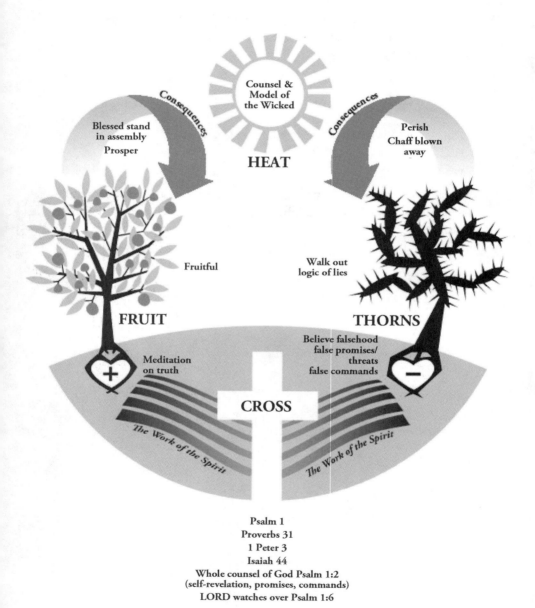

Counsel & Model of the Wicked

HEAT

*Consequences*

Blessed stand in assembly
Prosper

*Consequences*

Perish
Chaff blown away

Fruitful

Walk out logic of lies

FRUIT

THORNS

Meditation on truth

Believe falsehood false promises/ threats false commands

CROSS

*The Work of the Spirit*

*The Work of the Spirit*

Psalm 1
Proverbs 31
1 Peter 3
Isaiah 44
Whole counsel of God Psalm 1:2
(self-revelation, promises, commands)
LORD watches over Psalm 1:6

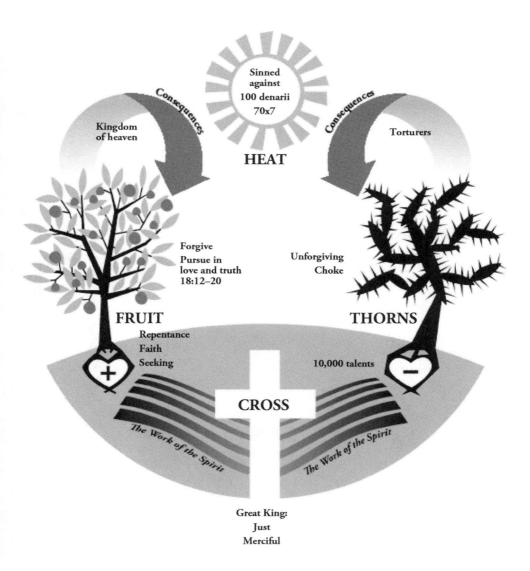

*Figure 4-7.* People Directly Wrong Us, Tempting Us to Return Evil for Evil (Matthew 18:15–35).

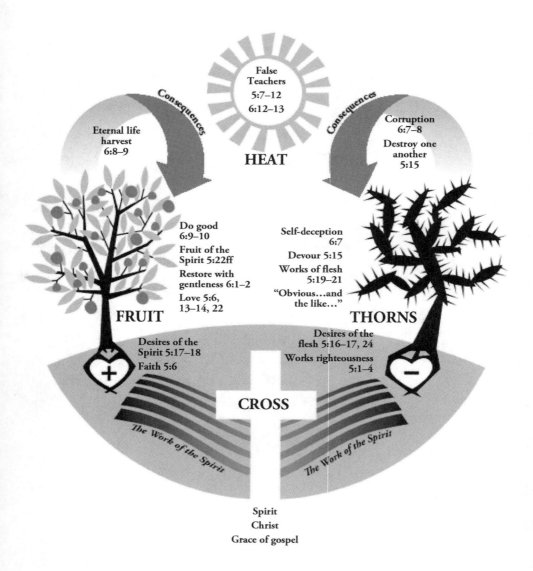

*Figure 4-8.* The Works of the Flesh vs. the Fruit of the Spirit
(Galatians 5—6)

False
Teachers
5:7–12
6:12–13

Consequences

Consequences

Eternal life
harvest
6:8–9

Corruption
6:7–8

Destroy one
another
5:15

HEAT

Do good
6:9–10

Fruit of the
Spirit 5:22ff

Restore with
gentleness 6:1–2

Love 5:6,
13–14, 22

Self-deception
6:7

Devour 5:15

Works of flesh
5:19–21

"Obvious…and
the like…"

FRUIT

THORNS

Desires of the
Spirit 5:17–18

Faith 5:6

Desires of the
flesh 5:16–17, 24

Works righteousness
5:1–4

The Work of the Spirit

The Work of the Spirit

CROSS

Spirit
Christ
Grace of gospel

**Figure 4-9.** What Is Biblical Change? (James 3:13—4:12)

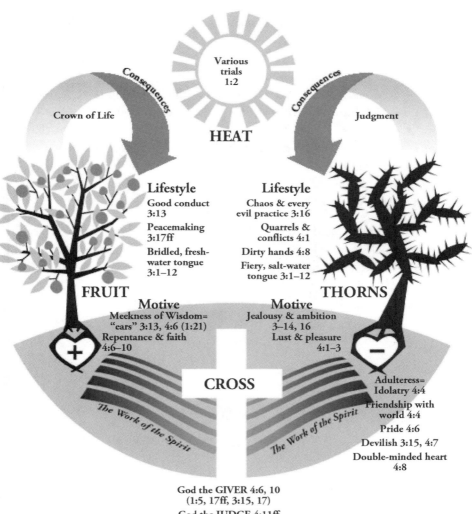

# Guide to Numbers 11—14

These chapters depict the pressures, temptations, and responses that Israel faced in the wilderness. As you look at these chapters, make the connections between the Israelites, the Corinthians, and yourselves.

- *Numbers 11:1:* The Israelites complained about their hardships before the Lord. They blamed him for their plight.
- *Numbers 11:4–6:* The Israelites complained about the diet God provided for them.
- *Numbers 11:10–15:* Moses complained about the people God had given him to lead.
- *Numbers 12:1:* There is division at the leadership level. Miriam and Aaron complain against Moses because of his wife.
- *Numbers 13:26–29:* The people complain about the fight that will be necessary to claim the land God had promised them.
- *Numbers 14:1–4:* The entire community complains about their hardships and begins to desire a new leader. They blame Moses for their problems.

The Israelites and Corinthians faced similar hardships. We, too, face similar trials at some level, hardships that touch on the basic issues of life, like food, shelter, good and bad leaders, and so on. How do we respond to them?

# HEAT 1: The Real God in the Real World

## REVIEW/DISCUSS HOMEWORK (30 mins.)

In your small groups, go over one or two of the charts (figs. 4-4, 4-5, 4-6, 4-7) and the diagram participants created using their own personal situation.

Also read Review, CPR, and the Big Question.

**Leader,** it's important to avoid two wrong ways to view suffering that Christians often fall into. The first minimizes suffering by not taking the time to understand how difficult another's experience has been or is. In this view, the sufferer only needs "to trust God" in order to handle their suffering. This view misses that God sees and hears the cries of the sufferer (Psalm 10:14) and that Jesus himself was a man of sorrows, well acquainted with grief (Isaiah 53:3). The second makes the experience of suffering central to the sufferer's life and identity, without reference to how God can use significant suffering to change us to be like him (Romans 8:28). This lesson is intended to help participants view suffering from God's merciful, understanding, and redemptive perspective.

## REVIEW

Let's consider what we have covered so far. In lesson 1, we discussed the promise and hope of being changed by God's grace, so that more and more we reflect the character of Christ amid life's struggles and relationships. Looking at this from the vantage point of eternity provides hope because, even when change is not occurring as quickly as we might like, we still know that God completes this work of change in us! In lesson 2, we saw that change is the by-product of being known and loved by Jesus, our Redeemer. Change is not accomplished by mastering a technique or following a system; it takes place as we are in relationship with Christ. In lesson 3, we saw that living in redemptive relationships with others (Christian community) helps us to see our constant need of communion with Jesus. Fellowship with Christ is foundational, but fellowship with others is also intended by God to be a crucial part in our spiritual growth. Lesson 4 introduced a model of the way God brings about change in our hearts. However, we can never isolate that model from the powerful impact of our Redeemer's presence in our lives, and the redemptive community—God's people—that encourages and supports us in the change process.

Lesson 4 taught us that God understands our struggles and can help us where we are:

1. God knows my world in detail (HEAT).
2. God understands my heart and how I operate (THORNS).
3. God meets me and changes me in the midst of life's challenges (CROSS).
4. God produces a harvest of good things in my life and the lives of those around me (FRUIT).

In lessons 5–12 we will look at these four basic elements in detail. We will start in this lesson by looking at HEAT.

## CENTRAL POINT AND APPLICATION

*Central Point:* God understands the full range of joys and sorrows that make up our lives.

*Personal Application:* Personal comfort and direction result from knowing that God understands my world and provides help that fits my need.

*Relational Application:* I want to help people understand that because God understands their struggles, he can offer help that is genuinely helpful.

# THE BIG QUESTION

What is your situation? What are your burdens, pressures, joys, hardships, temptations, responsibilities, opportunities, and pains—both actual and potential?

# LESSON CONTENT

**Leader,** use the list of possible answers below to help you guide the opening discussion. Write responses to be seen and referred back to.

- We tend to minimize how painful life can be.
- We expect life to be free of trouble, especially when we think we lead a good life compared to others.
- We think of good things and bad things as completely separate experiences, when, in reality, difficulty is often hidden in blessing and blessing is found in difficulty.
- We expect the good things we have to stay that way.
- We live as if we are invincible, thinking that we will have the biblical wisdom and strength to avoid or endure suffering. We are surprised when we don't.
- We are easily lulled to sleep by the advancements of modern technology, which may cause us to think that it can protect or rescue us.
- We place undue confidence in our plans and our ability to control our lives, and mistakenly think that we won't suffer.

## Opening Discussion (whole group, 10 mins.)

What are some possible ways to respond to suffering, and what assumptions do people make about suffering?

## DVD (17 mins.)

## Small Group Activity (10 mins.)

**Leader,** if you are not viewing the DVD, read Psalm 88 together before answering these questions.

What is your response to there being a psalm like Psalm 88 in the Bible?

Have you ever been in a situation or relationship where you felt all alone, and you wondered if anybody would understand what you were going through? Have you ever hidden a struggle because you were afraid of what people would think of you? Have you ever thought a problem was too big to be solved? In these situations, have you questioned whether God understood or cared?

## HOMEWORK

### The HEAT: God's View of My World

In lesson 4, we pointed out that God uses physical images to depict the world in which we live. The Bible says we are always living under the scorching heat of trouble or the cool rain of blessing. In either case, we are always responding to what is happening to us. One of the most refreshing things about the Bible is that it doesn't offer a sanitized version of life or our reactions to it. If the Bible left out stories of murder, rape, famine, disease, judgment, depression, and overwhelming fear, how likely would we be to believe that God's Word could help us?

It isn't pleasant to read about these things, but it *is* comforting. The comfort is found in realizing that I could never face an experience, no matter how dark or difficult, that would be a shock or surprise to my God. The hope and help he offers me reflect his deep knowledge of the full range of human experience. Because of this, some of the most comforting passages of Scripture may not even have the word *comfort* in them. Psalm 88 is one of those passages.

### Read Psalm 88

Consider the experience of the writer by putting yourself in his shoes.

 *1. Describe what you are feeling. (Support your ideas using verses from Psalm 88.)*

> vv. 3–5: You are in deep inner despair.
>
> vv. 6–7: You feel forsaken by God.
>
> v. 8a: You have lost your friends.
>
> v. 8b: You feel trapped and helpless.
>
> vv. 9–12: You feel like you are dying, crying out for help, but none comes.
>
> vv. 13–14: You feel as though God has turned his back on you.
>
> vv. 15–17: You feel like bad things always happen to you and nothing ever changes.
>
> v. 18: You feel like you wake up every morning to a very dark world.

Does it bother you that this psalm does not end on a positive note? Does it amaze you to consider that it was written as a hymn to be sung in worship? What can we learn from this?

- From the greatest joys to the most crushing sorrows, God understands the full range of human experience.
- The presence and promises of the Redeemer address people like us who live in a world where such things take place.
- God's honesty about these experiences invites me to be honest about the things I face. Biblical Christianity is never blind, indifferent, or stoic in its reaction to life.
- Going to God with my despair, doubt, and fear is an act of faith. Psalm 88 reminds me to run to God in these desperate moments and not away from him.
- The Bible is not about an idyllic world inhabited by noble people who always made the right choice. Rather, the Bible describes a world we can recognize, where good and bad things happen, and where people make wonderful and horrible choices. It is a world that makes us laugh but more often makes us want to cry. The Bible accurately describes our lives.

**?** *2. Are you like the psalmist? Are you able to be this honest with God? Or are you afraid to examine how you are responding to the HEAT you face? Are you hesitant about bringing the cries of your heart to the Lord? Do you feel like you have to put on a "good front" of unwavering faith before people? Does your Christianity honestly and powerfully impact the life you live each day?*

Psalm 88 is an invitation to honest and authentic faith in the face of chronic sickness, the burden of wealth, the rejection of friends, experiences of abuse, a fragmented family, the burden of single parenthood, the trauma of a crippling injury, the loss of a job, the temptation of quick success, a child's rebellion, a loved one's death, a church split, corrupt government, racism, perverted justice, the cloud of depression, the daily grind of work, and a host of other things that are part of life. We can come out of hiding with our struggles, and when we do, we will find that God already knows and understands.

### James 1:1–18

Another passage that breathes with biblical realism is James 1:1–18. Like all biblical passages, this passage loses impact when taken out of its historical context. In fact, it can sound callous and superficial until you understand the writer and his audience. James was a prominent pastor in Jerusalem. His congregation was in the midst of severe persecution that probably took place about the same time that Stephen was stoned in Acts 7 and 8. That background helps us to see James's words as caring, pastoral advice from someone very concerned about his congregation. As a pastor, James takes what he believes about God, his wisdom, and his comfort, and applies it to friends who are suffering greatly. Let's look at what he shares with them.

- *V. 2.* James gently reminds them that trials are inevitable ("whenever"—not "if"—you face trials). James knows that difficulties become more difficult when we naively assume that troubles won't come our way. Similarly, in Philippians 1:29 and 1 Peter 4:12, Paul and Peter urge us to realize that we live in a world where trials are a normal part of life. They are the rule, not the exception.
- *Vv. 2–4.* James begins to emphasize the blessings of trials. He has a strange way of talking about trials—he says that they bring us something we need. We tend to see trials as things we should try to avoid. But James says that without trials, we would remain immature, incomplete, and deficient in important things. Trials help us become mature, complete, not lacking anything!
- *Vv. 5–8.* In case you think that James assumes that trials are easy, and are to be endured with stoicism, consider his next bit of pastoral advice. James realizes how easy it is to lose our focus and perspective. He exhorts us to run to Christ for help and wisdom. We will find that God "gives generously" to the humble in heart.
- *Vv. 9–12.* Here James surprises us with the reminder that a trial can come in the form of a difficulty or a blessing. Poverty or riches can both be trials! Losing a job or getting a promotion, being rejected or receiving the praise of others, physical illness or

perfect health, are all forms of trial, according to James (and the rest of Scripture). Both present opportunities for temptation and sin as well as testing and growth.

- *Vv. 13–15.* This is why James shifts his focus from trial to temptation at this point. For James (and the rest of Scripture), a trial is an external situation (HEAT) that reveals the heart (THORNS or FRUIT). A trial can lead to significant growth at the heart level, or it can lead to temptation and sin. In other words, it can produce fruit or thorns. James says that it all depends on what is happening inside a person. If the trial leads to temptation and sin, it is because the person's heart has been "dragged away and enticed" by his "own evil desires." Nothing makes you sin; you always choose to sin.

- *Vv. 16–18.* Finally, James encourages his people by reminding them of the goodness, grace, and mercy of God in the midst of suffering. Our Heavenly Father is constantly pouring down his blessings on us. And the greatest blessing to come down is our Redeemer, Jesus, through whom we have been given new life!

What amazing, comforting, pastoral advice! James's words are full of grace and truth. He does not flinch at the reality of suffering but calls us to run to God. He warns us of cynicism and sin and points us to the God who loves us and has come to redeem us in the midst of our circumstances. Consider how it must have felt to have a fellow sufferer comfort you with these words in the midst of dire difficulty. What does it say to you as you think about a trial you once faced or face now?

? 3. *The certainty of trials, v. 2: What current trial has caught you by surprise? In what ways did the surprise impact the way you responded?*

? 4. *The benefits of trials, vv. 2–4: As you think about this particular situation, how can you see God using it to make you spiritually complete? What would you not have without this trial?*

? 5. *The need for wisdom, vv. 5–8: How has your prayer life changed as a result of this trial? Did knowing that God truly understood change the way you handled your situation?*

? 6. Two kinds of trials, vv. 9–12: How has it helped you to see that both difficulty and blessing are forms of trial?

? 7. Temptation and trials, vv. 13–15: What temptations do you face in the midst of a trial? How does this passage, with its focus on the individual and the heart, alter the way you think about your situation (HEAT)?

? 8. Avoiding cynicism, vv. 16–18: What has become clearer to you about the goodness and grace of God as you have gone through trials? Has your affection for Christ increased or decreased as a result?

Psalm 88 and James 1 both remind us that the Bible speaks of a real God who meets and comforts real people in the midst of difficulty in the real world. Psalm 88 emphasizes that God knows and understands what we are going through. James 1 provides an example of a pastor applying this truth to the lives of people he dearly loves. In both passages, the reality of the HEAT is acknowledged and responded to in ways that are truly liberating. We are not alone. God does understand!

## CPR

### Central Point

1. God understands the full range of joys and sorrows that make up our lives.
2. The Christian life is not about finding shelter from the real world as much as it is about God meeting us in the midst of it.
3. The Bible comforts us with the knowledge that nothing we experience is a surprise to God.

### Personal Application

1. Personal comfort and direction result from knowing that God understands my world and offers help that fits the struggles I face daily.
2. I must identify where I run from trouble rather than run to God.
3. I need to recognize the places where I miss God's comfort because I am embarrassed to admit my struggles to him.

### Relational Application

1. I want to help people understand that God understands what they face in a fallen world, and that he offers help that is genuinely helpful.
2. I want to help people to identify the false shelters that keep them from turning to God in their difficulties.
3. I can demonstrate the fact that God understands our struggles by modeling that understanding in the way I comfort others.

## Make It Real

1. Take some time to think about your life. What is the HEAT in your current situation? Use the questions below to make your responses concrete and detailed.

    a. What pressures do you regularly face?

    b. What are your God-given opportunities?

    c. What are your normal, everyday responsibilities?

    d. Are you facing difficult circumstances?

e. What temptations are you facing?

f. Who are the difficult people in your life?

g. What unexpected blessings have you received?

h. In what situations do you feel alone or misunderstood?

i. What challenges does the value system of modern culture present to you?

j. In what areas do you feel overwhelmed by the things that have been "assigned" to you (blessing or difficulty)?

k. Are there places where you are tempted to avoid, hide, or quit?

l. What situations tempt you to say you are okay when you are not?

2. Do you see any themes or patterns in your answers regarding relational struggles, responsibility, certain temptations, finances, physical suffering, and so forth? In other words, what part of the HEAT of real life tends to get to you? All the categories listed in question 1 are part of every life, but what things, specifically, tend to hook you?

3. Using one of the Bible passages from this lesson, write out a prayer asking the Spirit to help you apply what you have learned to your life and relationships.

# HEAT 2: The Real You in the Real World

**Leader,** it is important to allow ample time to discuss homework in each session. The Make It Real assignments are one way to ensure that this course is more than the dissemination of information. Each week Make It Real gives participants an opportunity to examine their thoughts in light of the lesson material. Be sure to give them time to talk about what they have learned and how God is changing them. This will also help you gauge how well your group understands the material and whether they need help with any concepts.

Reinforce to the participants the value of doing this study as a group. Talk about the way they can offer one another insight and encouragement. Remind them that others will learn from what they have learned and will be changed as they see God changing them. This curriculum is designed to provide a firsthand experience of the community of change it describes. This would be a great time to spend time in prayer as a group, asking God to help each person to meet God in a new way. You may want to divide your group into pairs, with each person committing to pray for the other person during the rest of the course.

## REVIEW/DISCUSS HOMEWORK (30 mins.)

In your small groups, discuss participants' answers to Make It Real questions 1 and 2.

Read together Review, CPR, and the Big Question.

## REVIEW

*Lesson 1*: Living with an awareness of God's commitment to heart transformation and our ultimate destination gives hope and perspective in our circumstances and relationships.

*Lesson 2:* The hope of personal growth and change rests on my relationship with a person, Christ.

*Lesson 3:* In addition to my relationship with Christ, God's work of personal transformation is intended to take place in a redemptive community.

*Lesson 4:* Practical hope, comfort, and direction in the change process result from looking at it from God's perspective (HEAT-THORNS-CROSS-FRUIT).

*Lesson 5:* God understands the full range of joys and sorrows that make up our lives.

In this lesson, we will take a closer look at the Bible's description of life in a fallen world and our struggles in the midst of it.

## CENTRAL POINT AND APPLICATION

*Central Point:* The Bible describes life this way: We live in a broken world as people who struggle daily.

*Personal Application:* I need to recognize the specific places where I struggle in a world that does not operate as it was intended.

*Relational Application:* I need to help others to be honest about their struggles with life.

# THE BIG QUESTION
### As God sees me respond to the HEAT in my world, what in me does he want to change? Where is God calling me to personal change right now?

## LESSON CONTENT

**DVD** (15 mins.)

**Small Group Activity** (20 mins.)
Read together 1 John 1:5–10.
1. How should we deal with our sin? How should we not deal with our sin?
2. What is God's response to our sin?
3. What then should be our response to the sins of others?

4. How does walking in the light lead to fellowship with God and with one another?

5. How can the truths of this passage encourage you in your Personal Growth Project?

Leader, this is what you want to learn to do and encourage others to do instinctively—to get to the heart.

1. admit to it, confess it, not keep it hidden, not ignore it, not claim it does not exist

2. faithful and just and will forgive us and purify us

3. not condemning; forgiving; leading them to seek Christ

4. Our sin separates us from God; we lack and hinder intimacy when we remain hidden and dishonest; by walking in the light, we have fellowship with one another because we share a common experience; we are drawing toward others instead of away.

## HOMEWORK

### The Real World: The Details (Romans 8:20–22)

The Influence of a Broken World

What three words or phrases would you use to describe the world? In Romans 8:20–22, Paul dramatically captures the essence of life on earth with three vivid phrases. They capture our everyday experience as we live between the Fall and the coming of Christ. Notice the three descriptive phrases.

1. *"Subjected to frustration" (v. 20).* This captures the futility you face in a broken world. You try and try but nothing seems to change. Your efforts seem to be for nothing. You wake up in the morning with a knot in your stomach because you know the problem is still there. This frustration exists in the big and small things of life. It whispers in your ear that all you can do is hang on. Where do you encounter this futility in your daily life?

2. *"Bondage to decay" (v. 21).* This phrase reflects the fact that everything is dying in some way. The bondage is in our inability to reverse the process. This reality is as close as our physical bodies. From the moment we are conceived, the dying process begins. The beautiful bouquet wilts and dies. Our homes deteriorate. Relationships disintegrate. Our spiritual lives drift easily into coldness and deadness so that God seems distant and the Bible

becomes boring. Where do you encounter the reality of decay in your daily life?

3. *"Groaning as in the pangs of childbirth" (v. 22).* No woman who has given birth can read this phrase dispassionately! While the first two phrases describe *what* life is like, this phrase captures our experience in the midst of it. Life is filled with intense struggle and pain. The image of childbirth reminds us that this pain is part of a process. *Now* is painful because *then* won't be. It is only because a child will be born *(then)* that a mother experiences pain *(now)*. The example of childbirth reminds us that there is redemptive purpose working in the midst of the pain; nevertheless, that does not make the pain go away. Paul is clear: there IS pain! Where are you experiencing that pain and groaning right now?

As you consider these verses, notice that Paul repeats a similar phrase in each one. He says in each verse that this frustration, decay, and pain are true of "*the creation.*" This all-encompassing category includes everything but God. The implication, therefore, is that everything else has been touched by sin and the Fall. Nothing around me functions the way it was intended. Everything is broken! When we consider what this means practically, we see some of the places where this brokenness exists:

- In nature, with storms, pollution, natural disasters, vicious animals
- In our physical body, with disease, weakness, old age
- In relationships, with conflict, division, violence
- In the mechanical world and its plane crashes, train wrecks, and appliance breakdowns
- In human culture, with its distorted values, racism, corrupt government, ethnic cleansing, and perverted justice
- In work, where "weeds and thorns" and all the matters mentioned above make labor more burdensome

## The Influence of the Evil One

On top of all this, the Bible adds an even more sobering dimension of reality: the existence of real, personal evil. Satan lives to tempt, trap, and torment humanity, and he uses all of the results of the Fall as tools to that end. He not only engages in direct attack, but in subtle, indirect attacks to thwart God's redemptive purposes in us and in the world. He is, in fact, "our enemy, prowling around like a roaring lion looking for someone to devour" (1 Peter 5:8). In the next verse, Peter includes the evil activity of the devil in the broader context of hardship (HEAT) when he says, "you know that your brothers throughout the world are undergoing the same kind of suffering" (v. 9).

## The Book of Numbers

### The Influence of Remaining Sin

When we watch a video we have filmed, we can easily see everyone and everything but ourselves, even though we were present behind the camera. We often tell the stories of our lives the same way. We can be conspicuously absent from our interpretation of our own lives. For example, a child tells his parents about an incident at school with little or no reference to himself. The parents learn a lot about the circumstances and the behavior of others, but very little about their child. But the Bible always finds the person in the middle of the circumstance and focuses on what he is doing. The Bible requires that I do more than simply get a picture of the world's brokenness. I must also focus on what I am doing in the middle of it.

### Lessons from the Wilderness

The Bible often describes life in this fallen world as a wilderness, where people struggle with their difficult circumstances. The exodus wanderings of the nation of Israel are obviously the chief example. In 1 Corinthians 10:1–11, Paul tells us that the lessons from those wilderness wanderings are "examples written down as warnings." They are intended to help us recognize ourselves and the typical ways we respond to the HEAT in our lives. Paul's point is that it is not enough to recognize the HEAT and suffering in our world; we need to know how we respond to it as well.

### Longing for the Past: Read Numbers 11:4–23

The startling thing in this passage is that the "trial" is relatively minor! It centers on a monotonous menu: manna. But the Bible doesn't just focus on the trial. It looks at how the people responded to it.

**?** *1. What were some of their reactions?*

*complaining, v. 1; wailing, v. 4; longing for an idyllic past, vv. 4–5; going after their leader, v. 13; rejecting the Lord, v. 20; questioning God's plan, v. 20.*

When we face difficulty, we tend to do the same things:

- We long for life the way it was before.
- We look for someone to blame.
- We question God's goodness, faithfulness, love, and wisdom.

In all of these responses, who is glaringly absent? We easily remove ourselves from the picture and blame our circumstances, God, or other people, forgetting that our hardship has been made even harder by our response to it.

## Fear of the Future: Read Numbers 14:1–4

This passage moves a step further from Numbers 11. If the struggles *within* the wilderness are overwhelming, the prospects of entering the Promised Land seem even worse! In Numbers 13, spies are sent to assess Canaan and what will be required to take possession of it. The people panic when they learn that even in the Promised Land, they will face different kinds of trial. In Numbers 14, what we see is all-out panic, as the people ask question after question about their future ("Why did we ever leave Egypt?" "Why is the Lord bringing this on us?" "What's going to happen to our wives and children?" "Wouldn't it be better to go back to Egypt?"). Don't we tend to do the same things when trouble comes? Consider these very common questions:

- "How in the world did I get here?"
- "Where is the Lord?"
- "What is going to happen to me now?"
- "What am I going to do?"

Have you ever asked these questions? They reveal a level of fear, doubt, and panic that complicates an already complicated situation.

## Anger at God: Read Numbers 20:1–5

Things continue to disintegrate. The Israelites are simply tired of trials. They are angry and looking for someone to blame. Moses is an easy target and becomes the object of their abuse. This passage shows us how quickly pain morphs into anger. The sick person who is irritable and agitated begins to yell at the nurse. The husband who concludes that his wife is not caring for his needs becomes bossy and demanding. The driver who has been stuck in traffic starts shouting at the one who cuts him off. This passage makes it clear that our anger says more about us and our relationship with God than it does about the trial. The Bible makes very sure that in the middle of a trial, the focus is on us!

**Leader,** this could be a good time to look back at lesson 4's three trees diagram and review it with the participants.

Read Deuteronomy 8:2–3

This passage in Deuteronomy shows us how to understand the wilderness wanderings.

 *2. Explain below how God used the wilderness wanderings in the lives of his people.*

# CPR

## Central Point

1. The Bible says that we live in a broken world as people who struggle daily.
2. The Bible reminds me that all of creation (everything I face every day) was broken and marred by the Fall.
3. God clearly depicts the ways that we, as sinners, respond to life in a world that is "groaning."

## Personal Application

1. I need to identify the specific places where I struggle with life.

2. I need to recognize where the brokenness of this world is particularly troubling to me.
3. Scripture welcomes me to be honest about the ways I deal with these difficult things.

### Relational Application

1. I need to be committed to help others to be honest about their struggles with life.
2. I need to lovingly help others recognize their expectations and disappointments as they deal with life.
3. I need to remind people that God welcomes them to be honest about the ways they deal with life's difficulties.

## MAKE IT REAL

### Personal Growth Project

This Make It Real begins a process of self-examination that will take you through the remainder of this course. This will be, by far, the most personally searching and rewarding aspect of it. What you do with this assignment and those that follow will determine how much you personally benefit from this course and how much it will prepare you to be used by God in the lives of others.

Your assignment is to choose an area of struggle from your own life. From now on, you will work on this area, applying what you learn from the HEAT-THORNS-CROSS-FRUIT model lesson by lesson. In the Make It Real section of each lesson, you will be given a guided opportunity to take the principles, perspectives, and promises of each lesson and apply it to your particular area of struggle. It is our hope that, as you do this, you will see measurable progress in that area of your life, while you get to know your Lord and his grace more fully and deeply.

Perhaps you are thinking, *I don't know how to choose the thing I should work on.* Here is some guidance.

- You may pick a relatively minor habit (biting your fingernails or breaking the speed limit), or you may choose a major pattern of behavior, thinking, speech, or emotions (a tendency to be shy and evasive around people, a tendency to be aggressive and controlling, or a tendency to judge or categorize people).

Either choice has its benefits. Small habits are easily observed bits of life that can lead you to think about more substantial issues. For example, biting your fingernails could lead you to consider how you handle stress and tension in general. Larger, more general themes and problems bring more of your life into God's light right from the start. If you pick a larger issue, like strained relationships with people, you will find it more helpful to narrow the focus, for example, by focusing on one relationship in particular.

- Here are some possible choices for a personal growth project:
  - *Driving habits:* your driving reveals a lot about your personality and expectations about life.
  - *Sports:* The way you play competitive sports is a window into your fears, pride, slyness, tendency to live on the basis of your performance, and so on.
  - *Money and possessions:* Are you obsessed with wealth? Fearful of poverty? Do you daydream about money? Are you selfish? Generous? Given to impulsive or compulsive buying? Covetous? Continually in debt?
  - *Work and rest:* Do you alternate between workaholism and a self-indulgent love of comfort? Are you driven and restless? Do you procrastinate and avoid responsibility? Do you pursue leisure in a way that pleases the Lord?
  - *Grumbling:* Do you tend to be negative, pessimistic, complaining, irritable, unhappy, discontent, and dissatisfied? When do you grumble and about what?
  - *Secret sin:* Is there an area of sin and temptation that regularly defeats you? Have you found it difficult to admit it and seek the help of others?

- Take time to pray. Ask God to give you insight and wisdom as you choose your project. Ask God to help you to resist the temptation to take the easy way out and give you the courage of faith to choose an area that really needs attention. Ask him to make you willing to be honest before him and others.

- Once you have chosen your project, write down everything you know right now about your struggle. When and where does this problem tend to rear its head? How long have you struggled with it? What have you done to get control or victory over it? What do you think Scripture says about it? How do you think it has affected you and the people around you? What do you think it reveals about you and what is important to you? In what ways, right now, do you think God is calling you to change in this area? Turn to the diagram in lesson 4 and try your best to answer these four questions:

- HEAT: In what situations and relationships does this struggle most often reveal itself?
- THORNS: How do you respond when the HEAT hits? What do those responses reveal about your heart? What are the everyday consequences of responding in that way?
- CROSS: What specific things does Christ offer you in your struggle? What promises can you claim? What passages speak directly to your struggle?
- FRUIT: In what ways does God want to change your heart? How will that heart change result in a whole new set of responses to the same old HEAT? If those changes take place, what will be the harvest of good consequences?

Don't be discouraged if you can't answer all of them, since your understanding will grow with each lesson. Be thankful that God has given you this opportunity to meet him and experience his grace, right in the middle of life's difficulties. It is our prayer that God will use this project to change and mature you and position you to be used by him in the lives of others.

# How Lessons 7–12 Are Connected

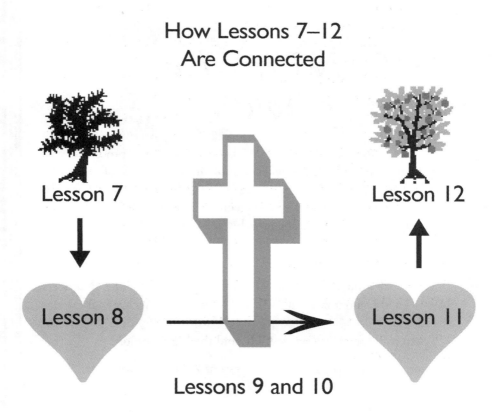

Lesson 7

Lesson 8

Lessons 9 and 10

Lesson 11

Lesson 12

# Lesson 7

# THORNS 1: What Entangles You?

The Make It Real section of lesson 6 launched you on a process of self-examination and growth that will continue through the rest of this study. You are being given an opportunity to use the most searching and hopeful truths of God's Word to take a life-changing look at yourself. This is the most important aspect of this course by far.

## REVIEW/DISCUSS HOMEWORK (30 mins.)

In your small groups, share your answers to questions 1 and 2 (Numbers 11:4–23 and Deuteronomy 8:2–3), and Make It Real questions at the end of lesson 6.

Also read together Review, CPR, and the Big Question.

**Leader,** use page 101 to explain how lessons 7–12 are all connected.

Lesson 7: Thorns
Lesson 8: Motivations
Lesson 9: Cross
Lesson 10: Cross
Lesson 11: Heart
Lesson 12: Fruit

## REVIEW

In the last lesson, we saw the Bible's dramatic and realistic portrayal of life in a fallen world and our struggle, as sinners, in the midst of it. It's not a pretty picture, but even this picture of difficulty and struggle gives us hope. We see that God understands the world that is so familiar to us.

His presence and promises meet us right where we live, and they are more than adequate to meet the challenges we face inside and outside of us.

As we saw in lesson 2, and as lesson 4 reminded us, Christ's death on our behalf and his presence in our lives have changed who we are. We are new creatures in Christ (2 Corinthians 5:17) even in the midst of a sinful and broken world that is full of HEAT! His power and promises are available to change us into people who know him, love him, and glorify him as we become like him. We all know that in the push and pull of life in this dark world, it is easy to forget the wonderful things that are ours as children of God. It's easy to have our identity more defined by our problems than by the grace of Jesus Christ. That's why it is important to remember that you already have new character qualities and behavior patterns that would not be in your life if you were not a new creature in Christ. You have already been given a new heart and radically changed by Christ's grace. You have already begun to experience the progressive restoration of your heart that is the focus of God's work in your life right now.

The only way to properly celebrate these realities is to humbly ask, "God, where are you calling me to further heart change? What heart qualities that you promised to your children are still not active in my heart?"

These questions will lead us to look at the THORN bush of figure 4-1 in this lesson. We will face the reality that although we *are* FRUIT trees by the grace of God, we still have thorn bush responses to life. The thorn bush represents the fact that, as sinners, we all tend to respond sinfully to the circumstances of life. We bend and twist the truth; we harbor anger and bitterness; we shift blame; we manipulate others to get what we want; we communicate in harsh and judgmental ways; we numb ourselves with business, substances, or material possessions; we attempt to get our identity from other people or our performance; we give in to lust, we give way to vengeance; we get defensive and self-protective; we respond selfishly and thoughtlessly—the list could go on and on. None of us is fully restored to the likeness of the Lord Jesus Christ, so there are shadows of all these things in our lives. This is why we are examining the thorn bush. As we compare the thorn bush to the fruit tree, we will begin to understand the specific ways in which God is calling us to further change. In other words, facing the ways we are like a THORN bush is one of God's chief ways of transforming us into FRUIT trees.

## CENTRAL POINT AND APPLICATION

*Central Point:* The biblical picture of the THORN bush captures how sinners tend to respond sinfully to the blessings and difficulties of life.

*Personal Application:* God calls me to an ongoing recognition and confession of my "thorny" responses to life.

*Relational Application:* Because we all suffer from spiritual blindness, it is an act of Christlike grace to lovingly help another recognize his "thorny" responses.

# THE BIG QUESTION

How do I typically respond to the circumstances
and relationships God has placed in my life right now?
What happens as a result?

## LESSON CONTENT

### Opening Discussion (10 mins.)

Read Ephesians 4:17—6:18 and list all of the ungodly, THORN bush responses Paul references.

**Leader,** as a large group activity, have the participants read through Ephesians 4:17—6:18 and list all of the ungodly responses that Paul references (twenty-seven behaviors). Remind participants that we never sin in general but always in the particular of our tone of voice, body language, eye rolling, words, and actions. Share with the group one way you have noticed this in your life.

### DVD (26 mins.)

### Small Group Activity (20 mins.)

1. What are some reasons why God wants to bring change to our lives?
2. Do you feel you can be honest about your own heart struggles with this group?
3. Do you feel the Personal Growth Project you selected is the one God wants to work on in your life?

Pray together for each other.

# HOMEWORK

Do you know that God calls you to be dissatisfied? Do you know that it is a good thing to be discontent? Do you know that you should be restless and hungry? The Christian life is a state of thankful discontentment or joyful dissatisfaction. That is, I live every day thankful for the amazing grace that has fundamentally changed my life, but I am not satisfied. Why? Because, when I look at myself honestly, I have to admit that there is still need for change and growth. I am not yet all that I could be in Christ. Yes, I am thankful for the many things in my life that would not be there without his grace, but I will not settle for a partial inheritance! I want nothing less than all that is mine in Christ! In this sense, God does not *want* me to be content. He does not want us to enjoy only a small portion of the riches he has given us. He calls us to continue to wrestle, meditate, look, consider, watch, examine, right, run, persevere, confess, resist, submit, follow, and pray until we have been completely transformed into his likeness. The Personal Growth Project that you began last week reflects that hopeful perspective.

This life of self-examination and joyful discontent should not be confused with a life of paralyzing self-condemnation. God does not call us to self-loathing but to a willingness to examine our responses to life *while* holding onto our hope as new creatures in Christ. That hope is not only based on the promise of forgiveness but on his promise of personal deliverance and restoration as well. The same grace that has forgiven me is now in the process of radically changing me. I must not be satisfied until that work is complete. Let's consider two "joyful discontent" passages.

## Read Ephesians 4:17—6:18: Don't Live Like a Gentile

This is one of Scripture's joyful discontent passages. Its contrast between the old and new ways of living is based on a celebration of the love of Christ (3:14–19), the reality of God's power within me through the indwelling Holy Spirit (3:20–21), and the offices Christ has established and the gifts he has given to his church (4:11–16). How do we celebrate all these wonderful gifts from Christ? By being committed to a lifestyle of joyful discontent, where ongoing self-examination and commitment to change are the norm. This is what Ephesians 4 is about. Let's look at it in more detail.

## The Lifestyle of the Old Heart

In verses 17 through 24, Paul sets up the contrast. The Gentile (old way, THORN bush) way of living is rooted in wrong thinking (v. 17) and wrong desires (v. 19) and results in the wrong responses to life. Notice the catalog: indulging in every kind of impurity (v. 19); lying (v. 25); destructive anger (v. 26); stealing (v. 28); unwholesome communication (v. 29); and fighting, slander, and an unforgiving spirit (vv. 31–32). The point is this: you cannot celebrate the wonderful things you have been given in Christ and at the same time be content with sin in your life. And yet the seeds of all these things still exist in each of us. We're at the beach and still plagued with impure thoughts. Under pressure, we still can play fast and loose with the truth. We allow ourselves to express too much anger with our friends, parents, spouses, and children. We might fudge on our taxes or "borrow" office supplies. We allow ourselves to say things we shouldn't or say legitimate things in an unkind way. We tolerate conflict in our lives. We slander reputations in thoughtless gossip. We hold onto offenses, unwilling to forgive. All of us need to continue to ask, "Where is the old Gentile way (THORN bush) still evident in my life?"

## The Lifestyle of the New Heart

In verses 20–24, Paul contrasts the old Gentile (THORN bush) way with the new "know Christ" (FRUIT tree) way. Notice that it is rooted in a new way of thinking (vv. 20–22) and a new set of desires (vv. 22–24). These new thoughts and desires result in fundamentally new responses: speaking the truth to your neighbor (v. 25); being angry without sinning (vv. 26–27); a lifestyle of giving (v. 29); and relationships that are kind, compassionate, and forgiving (vv. 30–31). If you examine yourself, you'll see that many of these good FRUIT responses are present in your own life as well. God *has* changed you. You *are not* what you once were. Yet, at the same time, the contrast Paul sets up in Ephesians 4 depicts our continuing need to be committed to new growth and change.

## A New Way of Living

What Paul does next (Ephesians 5 and 6) is apply this "new FRUIT" heart and the resulting "new FRUIT" responses to a catalog of typical human situations: our everyday relationships (5:3–7), our interaction with the surrounding world (5:8–14), relationships in the body of Christ (5:15–21), marriage (5:22–33), parenting (6:2–4), and the workplace (6:5–9). The point is that when I begin to humbly address my THORN bush responses, the results will be seen in the circumstances and relationships of my life.

Finally, in 6:10–18, Paul reminds us that this is what *spiritual warfare* is all about. The greatest war is the war for the heart (to be discussed in the next lesson). It rages in all of my situations and relationships. This is the war that Christ my Redeemer has already won by his life, death, and resurrection. I now have the right, privilege, and obligation to apply the spoils of that victory to my own heart and life, right where I live every day.

Because the Christian life *is* war, we cannot live with a peacetime mentality. Now is not a time for rest, retreat, and relaxation because we have not reached our destination. So, with an attitude of hope and trust in Christ, we continue to follow, fight, watch, and pray.

## Making It More Personal

The way to respond to the Bible's call to a lifestyle of joyful discontent is to look at yourself in light of the contrast between the fruit tree and the thorn bush we saw in figure 4-1. Consider the following questions.

- Where are your THORNS?
- Where do your actions, reactions, and responses not demonstrate the FRUIT of faith?
- Right now, in your current situation and relationships, how are you, a sinner, responding sinfully?
- Where are you experiencing the consequences of your responses?
- Where have you slacked off?
- When have you given in to anger?
- Where have you succumbed to envy?
- Where have you quit doing good?
- When have you spoken unkindly?
- Where have you tended to blame others?
- When have you accused God?
- Have you dealt with your feelings by doing unhealthy things (too much eating, spending, or working; escaping with too much TV or too many novels; too much emphasis on physical things like clothing, appearance, houses, cars)?

God calls you to come to this point. He calls you away from the wide-angle view to zoom in and humbly take a close look at yourself. He calls you to believe and act upon the gospel promises of forgiveness, restoration, wisdom, strength, deliverance, and power by acknowledging your responsibility for your responses to life. Getting to the fruit tree always starts with recognizing the thorns. The first step in planting a healthy, beautiful garden is removing the weeds.

## How Are We Dealing with the Obstacles in Our Lives?

We do not all respond to obstacles, temptation, suffering, and difficulty in the same way. We do not all respond to blessing, abundance, and success in the same way. This is because our responses are controlled by the thoughts and desires of our hearts. However, we can look at some typical ways people respond to life and organize them into categories. Where do you see yourself in these responses? Let's look at several THORN bush and several FRUIT tree reactions.

## THORN Bush Reactions to Difficulty

*Deny, avoid, and escape.* Here we pretend that things are okay when they aren't, and we pretend that *we* are okay when we aren't. We avoid anything that brings us close to our grief, and we look for ways to escape. Our escape may involve drugs and alcohol, people, work, overspending, or overeating. We may escape into gardening, TV, or community service. The point is that we are refusing to deal with what has happened in our lives and how it exposes the true cravings of our hearts.

For example, Frank is overwhelmed by the problems in his marriage to Brenda and the burden of parenting four young children. Although he maintains the public appearance of the happy Christian family, he increasingly finds it hard to face his responsibilities there. Work has become his refuge. Since he owns his business, he can justify the early mornings and late nights that keep him out of the house and provide an escape from the unending pressures he feels there.

*Magnify, expand, and catastrophize.* Here we give in to thinking that our life is defined by this one painful moment, that there is no good, truth, or beauty in our lives to make life worth living. We use suffering as the lens through which we view our entire world and see only pain, loss, and want. We convince ourselves that no one has gone through what we are going through. The larger our suffering looms, the more blind we are to the blessings we actually experience every day.

For example, although there is much she could be thankful for, Lisa is not thankful. To her, life careens from one problem to another. Lisa has had disappointments that many of us face in a broken world, but she has not borne unusual suffering. Yet that is how she views her life. She sees much more suffering than blessing, and she carries this negative worldview into each new experience.

*Become prickly and hypersensitive.* When we go through a difficult time, it is easy to see suffering where it doesn't exist. When we allow our hearts to marinate in anger and bitterness, we tend to become oversensitive and prickly. It's the "I've been hurt once and it won't happen to me again" syndrome. When we haven't taken the Lord as our comfort and our refuge, we become hypervigilant, scanning our surroundings for possible disrespect or mistreatment. This causes us to live defensively and self-protectively, always having our guard up.

Joan has been in many situations where she felt unappreciated. She is always on the lookout for potential disrespect. Recently, her boss asked all the women in her department to lunch—everyone *except* Joan. Joan was hurt and angry to be so publicly disregarded. The next day, Joan confronted her boss, only to learn that she had not been asked to attend because the boss was happy with her performance, but he had concerns about the rest of her department.

*Return evil for evil.* Here a person's life becomes swallowed up in malice, bitterness, control, self-pity, fear, self-righteousness, brooding, anger, envy, and vengeance. We meditate on how someone has wronged us and what we would like to do in return. Bitterness and an endless cycle of evil for evil complicate the problem. In the process, we damage our relationships with others and God.

Bill said it clearly as he talked about his unfaithful wife. "I'd like to see her hurt the way she has hurt me." He was unaware that this thought shaped all his responses to Jenny. The constant criticism and lack of cooperation that now made their marriage difficult every day were really subtle forms of vengeance.

*Bogged down, paralyzed, captured.* This is the person who quits in the face of suffering. He no longer pursues Christian friends, reads his Bible, or prays. His attendance at worship drops off. He stops volunteering for ministry. In light of what he has lost, nothing seems worth his investment, so he withdraws from godly pursuits, thereby exposing himself to even greater temptation.

Asaph said it best in Psalm 73: "Surely for no reason have I kept myself pure." Essentially, he is saying, "God, I've obeyed you and this is what I get?" Sometimes you look at life, and the good guys seem to be losing and the bad guys seem to be winning. You wonder if it's worth going on. There are times when we are paralyzed because what we face seems insurmountable.

*Self-excusing, self-righteousness.* In subtle ways I quit viewing myself as a sinner and blame the big sins in my life on others. As I lose sight of my own sinful heart, I become more intolerant and judgmental of others, and increasingly blame them for my own failures.

For example, Tom has a cold and distant dad. It *has* made life tough at home, but Tom's life has been made tougher by his own anger and rebellion. He probably won't finish high school, and he has already had his driver's license revoked; but when he looks at the trouble in his life, he lays all of his failures at his dad's feet, and, in so doing, makes what is already hard even more difficult.

We all need to confess that we have degrees of each of these reactions in us, if only for a moment. As sinners, we express a whole catalog of sinful responses to life. Growth in Christ results when we humbly examine our responses in the light of Scripture, looking for THORNS that may be growing in the heat of trials. We can be confident and hopeful even as we do this because of the grace that is always ours in Christ Jesus. James said it so well, "but he gives us more grace" (4:6). There is an abundant supply of grace for every THORN you identify, given so that your THORNS may become sweet and beautiful FRUIT!

**Lesson 12** expands this concept and talks about going to Christ in faith and repentance in a detailed way. But this should also be part of your discussion at this point in the study guide. Some people are overcome with their sins and become stuck in guilt and depression—going to Christ is the cure (Hebrews 4:14–16). Others ignore their sins or are oblivious. For them also, going to Christ is the cure, but they may want to start by praying that the Spirit will search them and reveal to them their hidden sins (Psalm 139:23–24 would make a great prayer).

We also need to recognize that each of these reactions flow out of our hearts. They expose what our hearts really think and love, what we really trust, and where we have placed our hope. In other words, these reactions help us to locate our particular god-replacements. (This will be discussed more in the next lesson.)

## FRUIT Tree Reactions to Difficulty

As we face our THORN bush responses, God never intends us to stop there. He calls us to repent, to receive Christ's forgiveness, and to rely on his power to replace THORN bush responses with FRUIT tree responses like these:

*Face reality.* It is right to experience the grief, sorrow, anguish, and pain that accompany suffering. Honest sorrow is the fruit of righteousness. Christianity is not a religion of numb, stoic, or callous people with artificial smiles. Jesus himself did not live a calm life without feelings. He wept. When it was appropriate, he felt anguish. It is never a lack of faith to feel sorrow when sorrow is the appropriate reaction to the HEAT we face.

Betty has not had a stoic, "praise-the-Lord-anyway" response to her divorce. Her days have been punctuated with tears, in an appropriate mix of deep sorrow over the destruction of her marriage and righteous anger over the offenses that led to it. She has not indulged in paralyzed self-pity or vengeful anger, but she hasn't been stoic either. Her mourning has been part of a biblical response to what she has suffered.

*Respond with appropriate intensity.* Sorrow, anguish, and grief must be expressed with the appropriate intensity. There is always something bigger than the heartache of this moment. Even if I have been betrayed or lost something precious, the most wonderful things in my life are not at stake. My relationship with God, my identity in Christ, the truths of God's Word, and the glory of eternity all remain secure and unchallenged. (See 2 Corinthians 4:7—5:10, where Paul compares today's suffering to present and future redemptive realities.)

George suddenly lost his job. His firing was unexpected and unfair. He was shocked, saddened, and angered, yet he also experienced an unusual calm and self-control. George understands that his employers can take his job, but they cannot take the most precious things in his life. Although he feels betrayed, he also recognizes that even in this difficult situation, there are many things for which to be thankful.

*Be alert.* Suffering is meant to wake me up from spiritual complacency. It is God's workroom, where he sculpts me into his image. Thus, it is a time for action, discipline, and perseverance. It is a time to experience in new ways all of the truths that I have professed are my hope.

It was amazing to hear Tamara say, "I am so thankful for this experience! I thought I knew God, but now I really know him. I thought I knew myself, but I realize I really didn't. I thought I trusted God's promise, but the things God took away from me were what I really trusted. I hope I do not have to go through this kind of thing again, but if I do, I know that it will be for a purpose. I was asleep and God has awakened me into action. I'm living with a purpose I did not have before."

*Constructive activity.* Actions taken in moments of grief and pain are often actions we live to regret. We panic and run away. We break a relationship. We forsake a commitment. We doubt God. We withdraw from people. We hurt ourselves. In some way we are always actively responding to difficulty. The call here is to do what is good. Seek God. Run to the body of Christ. Find comfort in the Word. Do the normal things God calls you to do. Ask yourself what rules the actions you are now taking: Are your responses shaped by a heart ruled by the Lord, or by the sheer panic of loss?

Through his suffering, Jim learned the value of the good things God calls us to do. Though he was tempted to give up, Jim got active. God's Word was his comfort. The body of Christ became his source of wisdom and strength. Times of prayer fueled every day. Jim took seriously what people said about him and became committed to personal change. He looked for solid Christian books and tried to fit regular reading into his daily schedule. He refused to be overcome and not only grew but ministered to others.

*Remember.* All of the hope and promise of the gospel belongs to you! In Christ, you have been made new! Because he loves you, God does not want you to experience just a portion of the inheritance he sent his Son to give us. He is working in every situation to finish the personal transformation he has begun in our hearts and lives. He will not stop until we are like him! Each day we should remind ourselves of the utter simplicity of God's comfort and call. First, God comforts us with his presence and power and calls us to *trust* him. Daily, we are to entrust to God the things we cannot control. Second, God calls us to *obey* and promises to bless us as we do. In good and bad circumstances, we must ask, "What has God called me to do, and what has he provided in Christ to enable me to do it?"

# CPR

## Central Point

1. The biblical picture of the THORN bush captures how sinners respond sinfully to the blessings and difficulties of life.
2. A practical faith in the gospel will give me courage to examine my actions and responses to life.
3. A commitment to get all that is ours in Christ will lead to a commitment to daily growth and change and a willingness to humbly examine my THORNS.

## Personal Application

1. God calls me to an ongoing recognition and confession of my THORN bush responses to life.
2. God does not call me to morbid self-condemnation but to a celebration of God's grace for my life and an attitude of joyful discontent.
3. Because the Christian life is a war for the heart, I must not live with a peacetime mentality.

## Relational Application

1. Because each of us suffers from spiritual blindness, it is an act of grace to lovingly help another recognize his THORNY responses to life.
2. As I call others to self-examination, I must remind them of who they are in Christ.
3. I must help people to look at themselves in the mirror of God's Word and not confuse my opinion with God's call to personal change and growth.

## Make It Real

1. Think about the struggle you have chosen for your Personal Growth Project. Use the categories from this lesson to identify where you may be responding to life in THORN bush ways.

Where do you see patterns of denial, avoidance, or escape?

When or where have you magnified, expanded, or catastrophized your struggle?

Are there situations or relationships where you are prickly and hypersensitive?

Are there situations where you are tempted to return evil for evil? As you face this struggle, do you feel bogged down, paralyzed, captured?

Where do you tend to be self-righteous or self-excusing?

Be humble and honest as you answer these questions, but don't allow yourself to become discouraged and overwhelmed. Remember, there is already evidence of good fruit in your life. The One who calls you to change has already given you everything you need so that those changes can actually take place (2 Peter 1:3–4).

2. Using one of the Bible passages from this lesson, write out a prayer asking the Spirit to help you apply what you have learned to your life and relationships.

# THORNS 2: Why Do You Get Entangled?

## REVIEW/DISCUSS HOMEWORK (30 mins.)

In small groups, share your thoughts identified in Make It Real. Identify, if possible, what FRUIT could be produced from these situations.

Read together Review, CPR, and the Big Question.

## REVIEW

In lesson 7, we saw the all-too-familiar examples of bad fruit that grows in our lives, even as Christians. That bad fruit (thorns), like good fruit, is rooted in the heart. Bad fruit—sin—is produced by a heart that has strayed from Christ and attached itself to something else. Real growth and change come only to people who, by God's grace, take an honest, biblical look at what is going on in the heart, beneath the outward, behavioral sins. Only then can you understand, appreciate, and apply the gospel so that lasting change can take place. In this lesson, we will consider what entangles us at a heart level. We will see the sinful, thorny responses (and their consequences) that spring from a heart ensnared by something other than Christ. This will prepare us to see what Christ-centered change looks like and how it happens, in lessons 9 and 10.

## CENTRAL POINT AND APPLICATION

*Central Point:* All ungodly behavior grows out of a heart that has been captured by something other than Christ.

*Personal Application:* If I am to grow and change as Christ's disciple, I need a deeper awareness of the things other than Christ that I tend to worship.

*Relational Application:* As I seek to help others grow, I must help them to see the motivations that produce THORNY responses.

# THE BIG QUESTION

### What has captured your heart? What cravings, desires, and beliefs rule your heart, producing ungodly reactions?

## Lesson Content

### DVD (21 mins.)

### Small Group Activity (30 mins.)

Read together the first part of Homework, below, to the end of the list of "typical responses." Share a time when you exhibited one of these responses when something did not go the way you hoped or planned. Is there a response that tends to characterize you?

Pray together for one another.

## Homework

Why do you sin? Why does a parent get agitated when a son or daughter won't do a few household chores? Why does a woman succumb to the sexual overtures of a co-worker? Why do teenagers become discouraged and angry when friends avoid them? Why do *you* do the things you do? It seems like such a simple question, but it really isn't. In fact, the way you answer *this* question will determine what you think the *solution* will be.

### Illustration

Let's take driving in traffic as an example. You are sitting in traffic and agitated. You look out your window and see a woman smiling and putting on makeup. Think of the many ways people can respond to something as common as being stuck in traffic. Here are typical responses:

- *Anger:* You will not be able to accomplish the things you had planned.

- *Happiness:* You did not get your makeup on, and now you have time to do that before arriving at work.
- *Anxiety:* You are afraid your boss will be displeased if you arrive late. It will impact your employment.
- *Relief:* You did not want to go to the doctor, and the traffic provides an excuse for missing the appointment.
- *Fear of man:* You promised to meet someone for breakfast, and you are afraid of what he might think of you because you are late.
- *Depressed:* You feel like there are always obstacles in your life. Things never go the way you think they should.
- *Guilt:* You think you should have planned better, left earlier or chosen another route. You feel like a failure.
- *Escapism:* You turn the radio on and eat an entire bag of candy to escape your frustrations.
- *You question God's goodness:* It seems like he is always singling you out and placing you in more difficult situations than he does others.
- *Envy:* You envy people who don't have to commute to work the way you do.

The list is endless! When we are in these situations, we are always seeking some explanation for why we respond the way we do.

What are some typical answers that people offer to explain and/or excuse the things they do? Consider these popular answers:

- *Other people:* "I would be a nicer person if you wouldn't treat me like that."
- *Family of origin:* "I act this way because I grew up in a dysfunctional family."
- *Suffering:* "I was deeply wounded by this event, and I have never been the same. I can't help thinking and acting this way."
- *My situation:* "I have had a hard day (finances, relationships, etc.), and you caught me at a low point."
- *Unmet "needs":* "I wasn't loved growing up so I am always living out of a deficit."
- *My body:* "I blew up because I haven't had enough sleep lately."

You could add many more examples to this short list, but these six areas seem to be the most popular places people go to explain why they do the things they do. While each of these can be very influential and should not be ignored, the Bible says that they are only the *occasion* for sin, not the *cause*. Problems in our background, relationships, situation, physical condition, and so on, can create the opportunity or *occasion* for whatever is in our heart to be expressed in our thoughts, words, and actions. They are the circumstances that bring our heart responses to the surface, but our hearts are always the *cause* of those responses and actions—that is where the spiritual battle is fought.

This does not minimize the significance of the things that shape and influence us, or the suffering we all experience. That is why we talked about the HEAT in lessons 5 and 6. Nevertheless, as we talk about the heart, this important distinction must be made because it will determine what you think the solution to your problem will be. It will ultimately determine who will receive glory . . . you or Christ! Think about the obvious solutions that correspond to these various explanations for sin. If these things were the causes of sin, the solution to my problem would be simple—and Christ would not be needed! For example:

- If other people were the cause of my sin, I would simply need to develop new relationships and avoid sinners.
- If my sins were caused by my dysfunctional family, I could distance myself from them.
- If my problem was suffering, I could seek out an endless supply of comfort.
- If my sins were because of my situation, I would change my circumstances.
- If unmet "needs" were responsible for my sin, I would try to get people to serve my needs and fill up what is lacking in me.
- If my body caused me to sin, I could get some sleep or other physiological help.

All of these solutions could be wise *aspects* of helping someone deal with difficulty and face life's trials and blessings. But on their own, they fall far short of helping someone change in a significant and lasting way. They are not adequate because they miss the central part of the problem: *They all miss the heart!* These solutions are external, so they miss the heart and bypass the centrality of the gospel. Christ is either unnecessary or just one part of the solution.

But the Bible says that my real problem is not psychological (low self-esteem), sociological (bad relationships), historical (my past), or physiological (my body). My problem is spiritual (my straying heart and my need for Christ). Ultimately, my real problem is a worship disorder! I have replaced Christ with something else, and as a consequence, my heart is hopeless and powerless. Its responses reflect its bondage to whatever it is serving instead of Christ. Let's look at some passages that stress the importance of the heart in relation to our sinful responses to life.

## Read Deuteronomy 5:6–21

Heart Idolatry: The Sin Beneath the Sins

The Ten Commandments may not be where you would expect to find this emphasis on the centrality of the heart, but it is there if you look carefully. The first three commands focus on what or whom you worship. They are a condemnation of making anything besides God your god! The order of the commands is important because our real problem is not our circumstances but our tendency toward idolatry. We have problems obeying commands four through ten because we have already broken commands one through three.

Consider the Israelites' situation. Their journey to the Promised Land was filled with trials, temptations, enemies, and suffering. And yet these realities were not of utmost importance to God. What was most significant to him was his people's heart devotion. He knew that the real war was being fought in the *heart* of every person who had been rescued from slavery in Egypt.

Look at the rest of the commandments. Why do you—and others—fail to keep them?

- Make God central in your worship and work (fourth commandment)
- Honor parents and those in authority (fifth commandment)
- Love, serve, and forgive others (sixth commandment)
- Maintain sexual purity (seventh commandment)
- Freely and joyfully share your resources with others (eighth commandment)
- Speak truthfully in ways that help others (ninth commandment)
- Rejoice in the blessings of others (tenth commandment)

The structure of the Ten Commandments teaches us that we fail to do these things because something is wrong inside us, not outside us. We wrap our hearts around something other than the living God and believe the lie that without that *something*, whatever it is, life is meaningless.

**Read Romans 1:25**

Good Things Morphing into Bad Things

This verse is essential for a proper understanding of heart idols. So often, we think of idolatry as worshipping and indulging in things that are obviously sinful. But according to Romans 1:25, idolatry is often the result of taking *good* things in creation and making them *ultimate* things that replace the Creator in our hearts and lives. When God created all things, he pronounced them "good." The creation is good in itself. But things can become idols in our lives if we misuse them by exalting them to God's place. Consider these examples:

- A father wants his young child to honor and obey him so that when he grows up, he will not be hostile to those in authority. This is a good desire and something God commands. But when this desire for respectful children becomes this father's ultimate goal, it has "morphed" to become his functional god. It leads the father to manipulate his son to get him to obey. The father may be very controlling, exploding in anger when the child steps out of line. He may become depressed and discouraged at any failure in his son or self-righteous, proud, and condescending toward parents whose children are less obedient.

- A young man longs for the day when he will find a spouse and marry. He reasons that this is something God created and a good thing to desire. But he is given to extremes in his relationships with women. He becomes depressed and susceptible to sexual temptation when women ignore him. When he does attract a woman's interest, he destroys the relationship by smothering her with too much attention.

- A woman is gifted and successful in her job. She recognizes work as a good thing that God has made, a place to use her gifts and experience a sense of dignity as she serves others. In time, however, this woman finds herself increasingly anxious about whether she is doing everything she needs to do at work. She starts taking work home, assumes too many responsibilities, and soon has trouble sleeping.

These people have taken something good—like obedient children, marriage, or work—and built their lives around it. God the Creator has been replaced by something in creation. When these good things become my functional god, they become idols. The worship of these "god-replacements" leads to THORNY attitudes, thoughts, emotions, and actions in the person's life.

## Read James 4:1–4

An Example

James 4:1 makes an obvious connection between idolatrous worship and ungodliness. When there is conflict between people, there is a war on the outside. But James concludes quickly that this war is an outgrowth of a war inside each person's heart. Desires are not being met, so people lash out in an attempt to satisfy those desires. In verse 4, James is even clearer about what is going on. He says that people who are engaging in ungodly conflict have begun to worship someone or something other than God. Something has become more important to them than God, and at that point they are guilty of spiritual adultery. Spiritual adultery is another way to describe idolatry. The person is giving himself to a false lover.

**Leader,** feel free to look at other passages where this connection is made: Luke 6:43–45; Matthew 6:19–24; Matthew 23:25–26.

This simple way of thinking about why we do what we do can have an explosive impact on a person's life. *It is explosive because understanding our heart's idolatry opens the door for us to apply and appropriate the gospel.* We know that God is committed to reclaiming our hearts through the work of Christ and the Holy Spirit. When you see your THORNS, your idols, your specific god-replacements, it shows you just where your heart needs transformation. It will lead you to hunger and thirst for God's grace. According to James 4:8, this is exactly the kind of person God loves to shower his mercy upon! Thus, a significant portion of growing in grace depends on your willingness to look at what fuels ungodly responses in your life. This negative side of the Good News must not be avoided because it leads away from THORNS to good FRUIT. Let's consider some tools you can use to grow in this aspect of your spiritual awareness.

## X-Ray Questions

1. What do you love? Is there something you love more than God or your neighbor?
2. What do you want? What do you desire? What do you crave, long for, wish? Whose desires do you obey?

3. What do you seek? What are your personal goals and expectations? What are your intentions? What are you working for?

4. Where do you bank your hopes? What hope are you working toward or building your life around?

5. What do you fear? Fear is the flip side of desire. For example, if I desire your acceptance, then I fear your rejection.

6. What do you feel like doing? This is a synonym for desire. Sometimes we feel like eating a gallon of ice cream or staying in bed or refusing to talk, and so forth.

7. What do you think you need? In most cases a person's felt needs picture their idol cravings. Often what we have called necessities are actually deceptive masters that rule our hearts. They control us because they seem plausible. They don't seem so bad on the surface and it isn't sin to want them. However, I must not be ruled by the "need" to feel good about myself; to feel loved and accepted; to feel some sense of accomplishment; to have financial security; to experience good health; to live a life that is organized, pain-free, and happy.

8. What are your plans, agendas, strategies, and intentions designed to accomplish? What are you really going after in the situations and relationships of life? What are you really working to get?

9. What makes you tick? What sun does your planet revolve around? Where do you find your garden of delight? What lights up your world? What food sustains your life? What really matters to you? What are you living for?

10. Where do you find refuge, safety, comfort, and escape? When you are fearful, discouraged, and upset, where do you run? Do you run to God for comfort and safety or to something else? (to food, to others, to work, to solitude?)

11. What do you trust? Do you functionally rest in the Lord? Do you find your sense of well-being in his presence and promises? Or do you rest in something or someone else?

12. Whose performance matters to you? This question digs out self-reliance or self-righteousness. It digs out living through another. Do you get depressed when you are wrong or when you fail? Have you pinned your hopes on another person? Are you too dependent on the performance of your husband, wife, children, or friends?

13. Who must you please? Whose opinion counts? From whom do you desire approval or fear rejection? Whose value system do you measure yourself against? In whose eye are you living?

14. Who are your role models? Who are the people you respect? Who do you want to be like? Who is your "idol"? (In our culture, this word is used for role model.)

15. What do you desperately hope will last in your life? What do you feel needs always to be there? What are you convinced you cannot live without?

16. How do you define success or failure in any particular situation? Are your standards God's standards? Do you define success as the ability to reach your goals? The respect and approval of others? Is it defined by a certain position or the ability to maintain a certain lifestyle? By affluence? By appearance? By acceptance? By location? By accomplishment?

17. What makes you feel rich, secure, and prosperous? What possession, experience, and enjoyment would make you happy? The Bible uses the metaphor of treasure here.

18. What would bring you the greatest pleasure? The greatest misery?

19. Whose political power would make everything better for you? Don't just think in a national sense. Think about the workplace and the church. Whose agenda would you like to see succeed and why?

20. Whose victory and success would make your life happy? How do you define victory and success?

21. What do you see as your rights? To what do you feel entitled? What do you feel is your right to expect, seek, require, or demand?

22. In what situations do you feel pressured or tense? When do you feel confident and relaxed? When you are pressured, where do you turn? When under pressure, what do you think about? What do you fear? What do you seek to escape from? What do you escape to?

23. What do you really want out of life? What payoff are you seeking from the things you do? What is the return you are working for?

24. What do you pray for? The fact that we pray does not necessarily mean we are where we should be spiritually. On the contrary, prayer can be a key revealer of the idols of our hearts. Prayer can

reveal patterns of self-centeredness, self-righteousness, material-ism, fear of man, and so on.

25. What do you think about most often? What preoccupies your thoughts? In the morning, to what does your mind drift instinc-tively? When you are doing a menial task or driving alone in the car, what captures your mind? What is your mind-set?

26. What do you talk about? What occupies your conversations with others? What subjects do you tend to discuss over and over with your friends? The Bible says that it is out of the heart that our mouths speak.

27. How do you spend your time? What are your daily priorities? What things do you invest time in every day?

28. What are your fantasies? What are your night dreams? What do you daydream about?

29. What is your belief system? What beliefs do you hold about life, God, yourself, others? What is your worldview? What is the per-sonal "mythology" that structures the way you interpret things? What are your specific beliefs about your present situation? What do you value?

30. What are your idols or false gods? In what do you place your trust or set your hopes? What do you consistently turn to or regularly seek? Where do you take refuge? Who is the savior, judge, controller of your world? Whom do you serve? What voice controls you?

31. In what ways do you live for yourself?

32. In what ways do you live as a slave to the devil? Where are you susceptible to his lies? Where do you give in to his deceit?

33. When do you say, "If only . . ."? Our "if onlys" actually define our vision of paradise. They picture our biggest fears and greatest disappointments. They can reveal where we tend to envy others. They picture where we wish we could rewrite our life story. They picture where we are dissatisfied and what we crave.

34. What instinctively feels right to you? What are your opinions—those things that you feel are true?*

---

* The x-ray questions were formulated by CCEF faculty member David Powlison as part of CCEF's course *Dynamics of Biblical Change* and are used by permission.

These questions can help you to think more clearly and deeply about why you do the things you do. They can help you get a better idea of which things typically morph from good to "God" in your life. These discoveries are a blessing, because they help you to see how truly lavish the grace of God is. The good news of the gospel shines brightest against the backdrop of our sin—so don't be afraid to look at these things. Take time to pray as you work through these questions. Don't lose sight of your union with Christ and God's promise to patiently love you and change you!

# CPR

## Central Point
1. All ungodly behavior grows out of a heart that has been captured by something other than Christ.
2. Often our hearts are captured by good things that have become ultimate things. Normal desires quickly morph and become replacements for God.
3. Lasting growth begins when we see the things that lead our hearts away from Christ.

## Personal Application
1. To grow as a disciple, I need to see that my real problem is my heart, not my circumstances.
2. I need to identify the good things in creation that I sinfully organize my life around.
3. To grow, I must recognize the things that can lead my heart away from Christ.

## Relational Application
1. To help others grow, I must help them see that their real problem is their straying heart, not their circumstances.
2. Biblical ministry involves a sensitivity to people's circumstances and a willingness to show them how even good things can wrongly take God's place in their hearts.
3. Assisting others to see the things that typically captivate their hearts is a powerful and loving way to help them grow in Christ-likeness.

## Make It Real

1. Another way to identify idolatry in your life as you work on your Personal Growth Project is to look for places where you evidence strong emotions like anger, fear, worry, and despair. In each case, ask yourself questions that will get you below the surface of your emotions. Ask yourself, "Is there something I want too much?" "Is there something I am afraid of losing?" "Is there something I am afraid of getting?" Take a recent situation when you experienced any of these strong emotions and write down what you might have wanted more than Christ. Do this in several different situations to determine if there is a theme evident in your life.**

---

** Questions 1 and 2 are based on material by Timothy J. Keller of Redeemer Presbyterian Church, New York City, and are used with permission.

2. Answer the following questions and look for common themes.

What things tend to function as replacements for God in my life?

What is my greatest nightmare? What do I worry about most?

What, if I failed or lost it, would cause me to feel that I did not even want to live? What keeps me going?

What do I rely on or comfort myself with when things go bad or get difficult?

What do I think most easily about? What does my mind go to when I am free? What preoccupies me?

What unanswered prayer would make me seriously think about turning away from God?

What makes me feel the most self-worth? What am I proudest of?

What do I really want and expect out of life? What would really make me happy?

3. Look back at lessons 1 and 2 and reflect on the promises taught there about God's faithful and persistent love for us in Christ. Take a moment to give thanks for the gospel and its specific application to your answers to questions 1 and 2!

4. Using one of the Bible passages from this lesson, write out a prayer asking the Spirit to help you apply what you have learned to your life and relationships.

# Lesson 9

# *CROSS 1: New Identity and New Potential*

## Review/Discuss Homework (30 mins.)

In your small groups, share any themes that you identified from Make It Real question 1. Share, too, which promises and truths of God's Word have been encouraging you as you identify possible idols in your heart. If you are struggling to find a theme, share one or more of the answers you wrote down, and allow your small group to help you.

**Leader,** Make It Real in lesson 8 asked your students to do two important things. First, they were encouraged to look for the things in their lives that tend to function as God replacements. Second, they were asked to reflect on the promises of God's love in Christ from lessons 1 and 2. After (or during, if you are not using small groups) the participants have discussed their answers to lesson 8, remind them of the importance of always connecting these two perspectives. Remind them that looking at idolatry without looking at the promises of the gospel produces hopelessness. Point out also that looking at the gospel without recognizing how easily we can become enslaved to other things robs us of an awareness of our continuing need for the rescuing and restoring love of Christ.

## Review

In lesson 8 we saw that our THORN bush responses to life are the fruit of root issues in the heart. Even though life in a fallen world *is* hard, it is not the hardship that causes us to respond as we do. Rather, our responses are shaped by the thoughts and motives of our hearts. When our love for something in creation replaces our love for the Creator, we will have THORNY (sinful) responses to both blessing and hardship.

In this lesson we begin to consider the resources we have in Christ to deal with our heart struggles. What does the person and work of Christ give us as we battle against subtle, yet powerful idols? How is the CROSS the only place of hope when we realize that our greatest problems are inside us, not outside? How will our lives change as we step out into life with CROSS-centered hope? Second Corinthians 5:15 says that Jesus came so that "those who live should no longer live unto themselves, but for him who loved them and gave himself for them." The focus of this lesson is how this promise of new life in Christ delivers us from life-shaping, behavior-controlling idolatry.

## CENTRAL POINT AND APPLICATION

*Central Point:* Because Christ now lives in me, I have everything I need to respond in new ways to what I face daily.

*Personal Application:* I must consistently ask where God is calling me to respond to the heat in my life with a CROSS-centered perspective.

*Relational Application:* I must help others recognize the practical daily importance of remembering that Christ lives in them.

# THE BIG QUESTION

In what specific ways are you failing to let the CROSS shape your situations and relationships? What would change in these areas if you lived in a more CROSS-centered way?

## LESSON CONTENT

**Opening Discussion** (10 mins.)

**Leader,** for the opening discussion, ask someone to read Galatians 2:20. Ask participants to share their understanding or knowledge of this verse.

**DVD** (15 mins.)

**Small Group Activity** (20 mins.)

**Leader,** this could be done as a whole group to switch things up.

Share ways that you have seen God transform your own heart or others' hearts.

Pray for one another, and thank God for his transforming work in us.

## Homework

Do you realize that you are always measuring your potential? When your boss gives you a new assignment, inwardly you are measuring your potential ability to complete it. As you head to the home improvement store, you think about whether you can handle the repair job you have begun. As you enter your last months of pregnancy, you start wondering about the kind of mother you will be. As you prepare to ask your girl-friend to be your wife, you ask yourself if you have what it takes to be a good husband.

In life's little moments and significant transitions, we are always eval-uating whether we have what it takes to do what we are about to do. The way we measure our potential has a lot to do with the decisions we go on to make. If we think we don't possess what is needed to succeed, we will probably decide not to do the thing that is before us.

As you stand in the middle of your life today, with all its blessings and difficulties, how do you measure your potential? What things lead you to say, "I am doomed to failure; there is no way I can pull this off"? What leads you to say, "I think I'm ready to do what I have been assigned to do"? What do you use to measure your potential? Do you say, "Well, I came from a good family with good models"? "I've gotten a solid education." "I have the talents necessary to do this thing." "I have learned from past experiences." "My past successes indicate that I will be successful again."

For you, as a Christian, each of these things has value because you know that your Lord has been sovereign over every experience and rela-tionship in your life. In and through each of them, he has been preparing you for what he has called you to do. Yet, at the same time, this standard of self-evaluation tragically misses the core of your potential as a believer. For example, it misses how a Christian can feel unprepared and ready at the same time. It misses how you can recognize past failures and present weaknesses and still step forward to do things you have never done or do things in a brand new way. It misses why some of us can admit that we have neither good family models nor a successful track record, yet we still have the potential to do genuine good in our circumstances and relationships. It misses why Christians can have hope and courage to face the things they failed at yesterday, believing that today they can do new and good things. Family, education, talents, experience, and success all have value, but they miss the core of our potential as the children of God. This is what this lesson is about.

## Your Potential: The Indwelling Jesus Christ

In Galatians, Paul is trying to explain the gospel to people who had a corrupted understanding of it at best. Early on, he says something so wonderful that it is almost impossible to get your brain around it! He says, "I have been crucified with Christ and I no longer live, but Christ lives in me. The life I live in the body, I live by faith in the Son of God, who loved me and gave himself for me" (Galatians 2:20). Let these words sink in and try to grasp what Paul is saying. When you do, you will understand your potential as a believer.

Paul does not focus on the fact that the CROSS enables me to be accepted by God and adopted into his family. Though this is very important, it is not Paul's focus here. It's important to recognize this because many believers tend to think of the CROSS only as the *doorway* into relationship with God. Paul is saying that the CROSS *is* that doorway, *but it is so much more*! Notice also that Paul's focus is not on eternity. Yes, the CROSS guarantees us an eternity, free of sin and suffering, with our Lord. But, again, many believers have the tendency to think of the CROSS as an *escape route* from eternal punishment to eternal paradise. Again, Paul would say that the CROSS certainly *is* that, *but it is so much more!*

So what is Paul's focus? He wants me to know that the CROSS defines my *identity* and *potential right here and now*. Let's consider the three main elements of Paul's statement and how they demonstrate that the CROSS of Christ fundamentally changes who we are and what we are able to do.

### 1. The Redemptive Fact: "I have been crucified with Christ and I no longer live."

Paul is saying something more than that Christ was crucified for him or that the CROSS of Christ benefits him. He is saying that when Christ was crucified, *he* (Paul) was crucified as well! What does this mean? It means that when Jesus died physically, Paul (and all believers) died spiritually. Paul sees himself so united to the death of Christ that he can say, "I no longer live." What does this mean?

From birth, each of us was under the control and dominion of sin. The death of Christ was not a defeat but a triumph (see Colossians 2:13–15). In his physical death, Christ broke the spiritual dominion sin had over us. Look again at the words, "I have been crucified." The verb points to a definitive action in the past, with a continuing and permanent result. What Christ did *then* on the CROSS permanently alters who you are *now* and who you will continue to be. But Paul goes even further. He says, "I no longer live." Paul is saying that the changes inside him are constitutional—so basic to who he is as a human being that it is as if he no longer lives! Yes, he is still Paul, but because of his death in Christ, he is a Paul who is utterly different at his core.

When you grasp the fundamental nature of this change within you as a believer, you will begin to grasp your true potential. You *are not* the same as you once were. You *have been* forever changed. You *no longer* live under the weight of the law or the domination of sin. Christ's death fulfilled the law's requirements and broke the power of sin. You *do not* have to give in to sin. You *can* live in new ways amid the same old situations because when Christ died physically, you died spiritually. This constitutional change is permanent! Do you view yourself with this kind of potential?

## 2. The Present Reality: "but Christ lives in me."

And Paul is not done! It is not enough for Paul to say that the death of Christ made him new. He has something more amazing than that to say. He says that when he died, the old Paul was not replaced with a new and improved version of Paul but with Christ himself! He's not simply saying that the new Paul is better at controlling the sin in his heart. He is saying something more glorious and practically hopeful than that! He is saying that where sin once controlled, Christ now dwells and rules! Our hearts, once under the domination of sin, now are the dwelling place of Christ, the ultimate source of righteousness, wisdom, grace, power, and love.

Here is the gospel of our potential. It was necessary for us to die with Christ, so that he could live forever in our hearts. The old me has died, and it has not been replaced with a better me. The replacement is Christ! My heart is new because Christ lives there. My heart is alive because Christ lives there to give it life. My heart can respond to life in brand new ways because it is no longer dominated by sin but liberated by the gracious rule of Christ. That is why I have the potential for amazing change and growth in my actions and responses to life.

3. The Results for Everyday Living: "The life I live in the body, I live by faith in the Son of God, who loved me and gave himself for me." Here Paul drives home the present benefits of Christ living in our hearts. We live by a new principle—not the old principle of sin and death but the new principle of the power and grace of Christ who now resides in us. This is what Paul means when he says, "I live by faith in the Son of God." We no longer live based on our assessment of what we possess in strength, character, and wisdom (from family, education, and experience). We base our lives on the fact that because Jesus lives in us, we can do what is right in desire, thought, word, and action, no matter what specific blessings or sufferings we face. *Our potential is Christ!* When we really believe this and live it out, we start to realize our true potential as children of God. We start to see new and surprising fruit mature in our lives.

The Christian mom who speaks with patience when she once would have spoken in anger is experiencing the reality of Christ living in her. The husband who comes home from work and serves his wife, even though he is tired, is living in the power of the indwelling Christ. The friend who chooses to overlook minor offenses and stay in a friendship she once would have forsaken is choosing to live on the basis of "Christ-within-me" faith. What Paul lays out here is intensely practical. It has the potential to radically alter the way we live and respond every day.

**What Does "Christ in Me" Living Look Like?**

What will my life look like if I measure my potential based on my union with the indwelling Christ? What will it look like to face life's difficulties really believing that he lives within me, empowering me to do what is right? Let's consider three important areas of new and surprising FRUIT, the FRUIT of faith in Christ.

As we consider this FRUIT—these changes in our living—keep in mind that we are not simply listing the things we should do as believers but, rather, what we have been given by Jesus. The CROSS has given us new life, new wisdom, new character, new hope, new strength, new freedom, and new desires. The Bible summarizes all of these things by saying that Christ's work on the CROSS gives us a *new heart*. This means that when we think, desire, speak, or act in a right way, it isn't time to pat ourselves on the back or cross it off our "To-Do List." No, each time we do what is right, we are meant to remember that we are experiencing what the CROSS has supplied for us.

Because of the work Christ did on the CROSS for us:

1. We will live with personal integrity.

- We will always be ready to examine ourselves in the mirror of God's Word, seeking practical, biblical self-knowledge.
- We will embrace the fact that change is a community project. We will live with a sense of need and thankfulness for the help of our brothers and sisters in Christ, living open, humble, and approachable lives.
- We will be honest in our struggles. We will not put on a stoic Christian front but express godly emotions (every emotional capacity is "very good"): anguish, pain, fear, anxiety, jealousy, anger, happiness, gratitude, and anticipation. Each has a proper expression in a life of faith.

2. As recipients of grace, we will create a climate of grace in our relationships.

- We will forgive as we have been forgiven. This means having a merciful attitude about the failures and sins of others, based on the mercy we ourselves have been given. (Matthew 6:12–15; Mark 11:25)
- We will be ready to ask for forgiveness, freed by Christ from defensiveness, rationalizing, blame shifting, and other types of self-justification and self-atonement.
- We will seek to give and serve in tangible ways. (Romans 12:14–21)
- We will persevere even when we are tempted to run. Endurance, forbearance, long-suffering, patience, and perseverance are on every biblical list of the character traits of a new heart. The common thread is doing what is right even when the HEAT remains.

3. We will act with courageous grace and constructive truth.

- We will speak with honesty and candor in the pursuit of blessing and peace. (Leviticus 19:17; Ephesians 4:29)
- We will gladly forgive anyone who seeks it. (Luke 17:1–10; Ephesians 4:30—5:2)
- We will be committed to having our responses more shaped by the will of the Savior than our own selfish desires, the demands

and expectations of others, or the pressures of the situation. The grace of Christ at work in our hearts enables us to say no to these things, so that we can say yes to his call.

Each of these will be developed in more detail in lesson 12.

# CPR

## Central Point
1. Because I died with Christ, sin's dominion over me has been broken.
2. My heart, once controlled by sin, is now the dwelling place of the Lord Jesus Christ.
3. I now live by a new principle: the principle of the grace and power of Christ who lives within me.

## Personal Application
1. I must remember that I am not the same as I once was. I have been forever changed by Christ's work on the CROSS.
2. I have potential for amazing change and growth because Christ lives within me.
3. Because Christ lives within me, I have his wisdom, strength, and character at my disposal.

## Relational Application
1. I want to help others recognize that the CROSS guarantees that they are constitutionally changed; they are not what they once were.
2. I want to help others grasp the hope and potential that is theirs because Christ lives within them.
3. I want to help others recognize where they have failed to live out of the wisdom, strength, and character that is theirs in Christ.

# MAKE IT REAL

Here is another opportunity to examine the area you chose as your Personal Growth Project. Think about what you have learned about life in this fallen world, your own heart and behavior, the consequences of your choices and actions, and now, the amazing heart- and life-changing grace of the Lord Jesus. As you reflect on what you have learned, begin thinking about how the CROSS equips you to deal with your struggle. Use these questions to guide your thoughts.

1. Where have you failed to recognize that sin's power over you has been broken, and you do not have to give in to it any longer? How would embracing this truth change the way you think and respond?

2. Where have you failed to live up to your full potential as a child of God? Where have you failed to take advantage of the wisdom, strength, and character that is yours because Christ lives within you? In what specific situations and relationships do you have God-given opportunities to exercise the new things that are yours in Christ?

3. Where have you been repeatedly tempted to forget that the cross has fundamentally changed you, which has led you to give in to old temptations and patterns? How would remembering the cross lead to new ways of dealing with these old things?

4. Where, specifically, would a cross-centered perspective change your relationships? (Forgiveness? Patience and grace? Compassion and gentleness? Making peace? Speaking the truth? Humble service? Saying no?)

5. Where is God calling you to new ways of living in the middle of the same old stuff? Where do you need to say, "I do not have to give in to that!" or "I have greater potential than that!"

6. Using one of the Bible passages from this lesson, write out a prayer asking the Spirit to help you apply what you have learned to your life and relationships.

# CROSS 2: The Cross and Daily Living

## REVIEW/DISCUSS HOMEWORK (30 mins.)

In small groups, share your answers to Make It Real questions 1–5.

Review the At a Glance picture, and explain the importance and relevance of the three points in the Foundation. Read CPR and the Big Question.

## CENTRAL POINT AND APPLICATION

*Central Point:* Living CROSS-centered lives that transform us into the likeness of Christ is the result of repentance and faith that looks deeply at sin alongside the magnificent grace of Christ.

*Personal Application:* To live a CROSS-centered life, I need to exercise a repentance and faith that see the depth of my waywardness and the power and glory of my Redeemer.

*Relational Application:* Helping others live CROSS-centered lives involves helping them to see their ruling idolatries alongside the superiority of Christ.

## THE BIG QUESTION

Who are you? What is your new identity?
How does believing this help you to identify and repent
of the heart sins beneath your behavioral sins? How does it help you
move in new directions that are pleasing to God?

## LESSON CONTENT

**DVD** (21 mins.)

**Small Group Activity** (30 mins.)

**Leader,** invite someone from the study (if possible) to lead the whole group in a time of worship, which can include songs, prayers of confession and forgiveness, prayers of praise and thanksgiving, Scripture reading, and so on.

## HOMEWORK

In lesson 9, we saw the amazing reality of God's work of regeneration—the way Christ's death for your sins makes you a new creature with a new heart. The old has gone and the new has come (2 Corinthians 5:17)! This is true the moment you turn from your sin and embrace Christ. This amazing transformation is *already* true of you. It is who you really are *now*, the *real* you. In lesson 1, we considered the great hope of our eventual and inevitable glorification and what we will be one day when we are completely changed into the likeness of Christ. The point of lesson 9 is that the process has already begun and—in terms of our standing before God—is already complete!

But if this is true, why do Christians still struggle so much with sin? How do we get so bogged down that it feels like nothing has changed and nothing is new? That is what this lesson discusses. We will square off with the fact that, while many new things are already true of us in Christ, and one day we will be like him, *right now* there is much that is incomplete. This is why we need to keep the CROSS of Christ central as we live the Christian life every day.

### The Cross-centered Life

What do we mean by a CROSS-centered life? Let's start by thinking about it this way. All people live their lives based upon some identity, some sense of who they are. They get up in the morning with some definition of who they are, what they are like, and what they are worth. Many people are not particularly aware of their view of themselves, but it nevertheless determines how they respond to everything they will face during the day. It influences their responses to every challenge and opportunity.

Lesson 9 showed us that the Christian is meant to define himself as a new creation in Christ. The Christian is new on the inside. The heart of stone has been replaced with a heart of flesh. This lesson will elaborate on who you are in Christ. It will also explain how seeing *and* believing this enables you to grow in grace as you repent of sin. The Christian has quite a CROSS-centered perspective of himself, defining himself in terms of what Christ's life, death, and resurrection have made him to be.

This is important because many Christians have very little idea of what it means to live a CROSS-centered life. What about you? How much of the way you view yourself is shaped by what Jesus did for you on the CROSS? Do you know what it means to live a CROSS-centered life and what it looks like on a daily basis? A good number of Christians think that the CROSS is what you need in order to *become* a Christian. They think, *I need forgiveness and Christ's righteousness to begin the Christian life, but once I am a Christian, I need to get to work and follow Christ's example of holiness.* The tricky thing about this perspective is that it is partially correct! Once you have become a Christian, you *do* participate in your ongoing growth. You *do* actively pursue the obedience of faith. You *do* make an effort and engage in spiritual warfare! However, you are never meant to minimize your *continuing* need for the CROSS of Christ in the process of becoming holy—like Christ.

## Illustration

Consider Joe, who became a Christian five years ago. For the first three years, Joe woke up early every morning to pray and read his Bible for an hour. He faithfully sought out fellowship with other Christians and shared his new faith regularly. But for the past two years, Joe has struggled with guilt. He has grown distant from his Christian friends and lost his incentive to talk to others about Christ. In addition, Joe has begun to struggle with overeating. Occasionally he will visit Internet sites and randomly buy needless items online. He says it cheers him up when he is down. In other words, Joe is slipping back into habits that dominated him before he became a Christian.

Joe's friends say that his problems started about the same time he missed his first quiet time. Therefore, Joe has redoubled his efforts to read his Bible and pray, but it just doesn't seem the same. The Bible seems dull, and his mind wanders when he prays. What has gone wrong with Joe? Most would conclude, like Joe's friends, that Joe has grown lazy and that he is not using the things God has provided to help him grow: the Bible, prayer, fellowship, ministry, and service. And it's true: these *are* factors that have contributed to Joe's slow downward spiral.

But Joe's problem is much deeper than that. In fact, his problems started long before he missed his first quiet time. What happened is that Joe lost sight of his ever-present need for the CROSS of Christ almost as soon as he became a Christian. If you had known Joe during the first three years of his Christian life, when he was faithfully engaging in the basic Christian disciplines, you would have met a confident man who quickly rebuked others who struggled with their personal devotions or witnessing.

Although Joe had *come* to Christ acknowledging that he was lost and without hope except for the mercy of Christ, he quickly began to live as if *progress* in the Christian life was up to him. "Jesus got me in; I have to do the rest" was Joe's functional identity. "It's all up to me." For the first three years, he was proud because he was working hard to grow and moving ahead successfully. He was confident because of his own efforts and accomplishments. He saw very little need for the CROSS of Christ because he had *already* been forgiven and was now forging ahead in the Christian life. His sense of acceptance before God had quickly shifted from what Christ had done for him to what he was doing for Christ! And because he was successful, he tended to be proud, self-righteous, and judgmental toward those less faithful and disciplined, and defensive when criticized.

In the past two years, the external behaviors have changed, but the problem is the same. Instead of being proud of his righteous efforts, Joe is ashamed, guilty, depressed at times, and easily attracted by old temptations. He feels like a failure because he can no longer keep up the routine. What is Joe's real problem? In both phases of Joe's Christian life, Christ's work on the CROSS was radically minimized or replaced by Joe's own efforts. The first three years evidenced Christless activism, which produced pride and self-sufficiency. This may not look all that bad on the outside, but it is as dangerous as Joe's recent behavior of Christless passivity, which has produced guilt, depression, and a host of bad habits.

The sad fact is that Joe is not that unusual. Many Christians begin the Christian life with a clear understanding of their need for Christ but quickly lose sight of how central Christ must be *throughout* it. If Joe had kept the CROSS central in those first three years of his Christian life, he could have avoided pride and self-righteousness. The CROSS would have daily reminded him that anything good in his life was because of Christ's grace and power at work in him. He also could have handled the failures of the past two years. The CROSS would have daily reminded him that, though he is weak, Christ has given him a new identity and a safe place to deal honestly with sin.

In what ways have you experienced a similar attitude as Joe?

## FAITH AND REPENTANCE ARE THE KEY

How do you avoid leading a CROSSless life? The answer is found in moment-by-moment faith and repentance. Faith keeps us holding on to the grace and mercy of Christ and thereby avoiding despair. Repentance keeps us facing our ongoing struggle with sin and thereby avoiding pride. This is just what Joe needs—throughout his Christian life. This is what every Christian needs. And yet so many Christians only think of faith and repentance as the way you initially enter the Christian life. They fail to realize that faith and repentance must continue throughout the Christian life. Faith and repentance enable us to fight sin because they link us to Christ on a moment-by-moment basis. Faith is another way of saying, "seeing Christ's glory and grace and turning to him." Repentance is another way of saying, "admitting and turning from sin." They are two sides of the same coin. Both are essential for change in the Christian life. Both are essential if we are going to keep the CROSS of Christ central!

### Faith: Seeing Who You Are in Christ, 1 John 2:1–2; 3:1–3

Repentance, or turning from sin, is never easy—it means admitting that you are wrong! Something in every human heart avoids this. When was the last time you had to admit that you were wrong and ask someone to forgive you? What was most difficult? No doubt your own pride was a major stumbling block. There may also have been fear that the other person would not forgive you—and would possibly use your confession against you.

But what if you *knew* that the person would be welcoming and full of joy? Wouldn't that make admitting you were wrong and asking for forgiveness an incredibly freeing experience? Of course it would! In 1 John, a letter that calls us to self-examination and holiness, we also find rich pictures of who we are in Christ. Seeing Christ is essential if we are going to admit to and turn from our sin. First John teaches us that we are new on the inside due to a new birth (2:29), the profound truth we considered in lesson 9. First John also teaches that we are going to be completely changed one day (3:2), which we studied in lesson 1. First John also says that we have a new status—we have been justified and adopted. All of these elements are critical as we live the Christian life. We cannot minimize any of them. In this lesson we are focusing on our new legal status. Seeing this will make us eager to repent and pursue holiness. (You may also look at Paul's prayers in Ephesians 1:15–23 and 3:14–19 to show how concerned Paul is about keeping Christ and the CROSS central in the believer's daily life.)

You Are Justified

Read 1 John 2:1–2

In 1 John 2:1–2, we have a clear description of our justification. This brief passage summarizes the foundation of our justification:

- *Verse 1:* Christians continue to struggle with sin. John refers to his readers as his children in the faith. They are Christians in whom he longs to see progress in holiness. But sin is still a reality in their lives. (We looked at this in detail in lessons 7 and 8.) Our need for the cross is not over!
- *Verse 1:* Jesus is our defense lawyer. John says that when we sin, Jesus speaks to the Father on our behalf and defends us, saying that we should not be punished for our sins. They have already been atoned for, and we are legally righteous in Christ. He says something like this: "Father, I know that _____ has sinned and that change needs to happen in his life. But it would be unjust for you to try him for this sin and to convict him and condemn him. You would be punishing two people for the same sin—him and me. That would be unjust of you, Father." First John 1:9 says that when we confess our sins, God is faithful

and just to forgive us. He is just to forgive us because Jesus has already made atonement for that sin. Jesus is able to make a strong case for us because of who he is and what he has done for us. Verses 1 and 2 say he has done two things:

1. He has atoned for our sins. He paid the penalty we deserved by dying the death we should have died for our sins.

2. He has given us a legally righteous standing before the Father, based on his life of perfect obedience. He is the Righteous One who lived the life we should have lived.

The amazing thing about our justification that many Christians fail to see and apply is this: God not only forgives you because Christ has paid for your sins, he also treats you as if you had fully and perfectly obeyed the law because Christ obeyed it perfectly for you. *He is your righteousness.* This is truly mind-boggling!

You Are Adopted

Read 1 John 3:1–3

As if our justification were not enough, God has done even more! In 1 John 3:1–2, we find a vivid description of our adoption. This passage keeps the critical truth of our adoption before us.

- *Verse 1:* Christians have a radical new relationship with God. Because we have been justified, we are welcomed into the presence and family of God. God is no longer our judge; he is our father. In this verse, John's joy spills over because God has done more than justify us. We see this in three ways:

    1. Though not evident in most translations, John begins verse 1 with "*Behold.*" He is saying, "Stop and think about this! Don't miss this incredible truth."

    2. The phrase translated "How great" literally means "from what country." A modern interpretation of this phrase would be "from what planet"! The Father's love is so immense that it is hard to conceive of where it could originate except in God himself.

    3. When John says, "And that is what we are," he can hardly contain himself. He is saying, "Can you believe it? We have not just been justified; we have been made God's children. What amazing love!"

- *Verses 2–3:* This amazing love of the Father compels us to live for him. This love, when rightly understood, will inevitably propel you in the direction of holiness and growth in grace. This order is essential: I am a new creation, fully accepted, adopted, and free; *therefore* I want to please God. We do NOT say: I will try to please God *so that* I may become a new creation, make myself acceptable, and hope that God adopts me and sets me free!

*This is who you are!* This is how you are to think of yourself daily. You are dead to sin (lesson 9) and in a new relationship with the Father because of what Christ has done for you on the CROSS (lesson 10). Father, Son, and Holy Spirit have done something truly amazing. They have made it possible for sinners to draw near! What should this produce in the Christian? A deep gratitude and a new confidence to look honestly at our sin and repent daily.

## Repentance: Admitting and Turning from Sin

Read Luke 15:11–32

If a Christian is grounded in this new identity, it will show itself in a life of repentance. The Bible gives us a picture of what faith and repentance look like when the ugliness of sin and the beauty of the CROSS are fully understood and believed. In the story of the Prodigal Son in Luke 15:11–32, we see three essential ingredients in faith-driven repentance.

### 1. Wake Up: "He came to his senses" (v. 17)

For lasting change to take place, you must *see* that your biggest problem is you, not your circumstances. No matter how difficult things may be, your deepest need is to know and be known by God. In the case of the prodigal son, it took difficulty and poverty to awaken him to his true condition. Isn't it often the HEAT that God uses to bring us to self-awareness? What begins as very shallow repentance grows and deepens. You start to wake up to many things, like those listed below. When these things happen, change is beginning!

- You see life as a moral drama of immense proportions. "How will I live?"
- You have a new sobriety about life and the reality of sin, suffering, and the need for grace.
- Momentary pleasures and distractions no longer hold your attention. This is the life breath of which biblical repentance breathes.

- Biblical truth begins to make sense as you think about your situation.
- The Bible gets personal. It has your name on it.
- You begin to make connections between your heart and behavior.
- You begin to see that God is a God of grace and mercy. He begins to get attractive.

## 2. Own Up: "He admitted his sin" (v. 18)

The wake-up call is followed by the deep work of true repentance. If this is happening, we will not treat God's grace lightly. Three things are involved.

- *Godly, not worldly, sorrow.* The prodigal son saw that his sin was against his father and heaven. This is godly sorrow as opposed to worldly sorrow (see 2 Corinthians 7:10). Worldly sorrow is only being sorrowful because you were caught or because you failed to live up to your own standards and potential or because you are experiencing the consequences of your sin. Worldly sorrow is self-centered, while godly sorrow focuses on how God was offended and others were hurt. Godly sorrow especially sees that God's love (not just his commands) has been treated lightly. Worldly sorrow produces tears of self-pity, but godly sorrow produces tears of true humility.
- *Seeing the sin beneath the sins.* You begin to see the heart sins beneath your behavioral sins, the idolatrous lies that drive you to do what you are doing. Remember, before you violate commandments 4 through 10, you violate commandments 1 through 3 by forsaking the love of God for something else. Repentance shows you how spiritually blind you have been. There is no more excuse-making or blame-shifting; instead, there is honest self-examination. You can be self-critical without getting defensive or depressed.
- *Repenting of sin AND righteousness.* You start repenting of your righteousness and not just your sins. What does this mean? Every time we try to build our lives on what *we* try to do or be *apart from Christ,* it is an attempt to justify ourselves. It is a way we try to create a righteousness apart from Christ so that we can feel accepted before God, others, and ourselves. A Christian not only sees the THORNY behavior that results from these false

identities; he also sees the many "good" things that may have been motivated by the worship of something besides the true God. He repents of those things as well.

For example, suppose you do not feel accepted by God, others, or yourself unless you are doing something for someone. You are placing your hopes for acceptance not on Christ, but on an identity that will make you look like a truly sacrificial person. Repentance will lead you to repent of such sacrificial efforts because they cannot make you right with God.

### 3. Shift Weight: "He ran into his father's gracious embrace" (v. 20)

When you admit the depth of your sin and repent, as the prodigal son did, the love of the Father, Son, and Holy Spirit begins to get attractive. The false identities and idols that were once so alluring lose their appeal. You start to experience the love of Christ, and when this happens, change follows. Notice how prominent the father's lavish love is in this story. The father runs toward the humble and repentant son. What does this tell us about what true repentance looks like?

- You begin to rest in Christ's work as you confess your sins, asking for forgiveness and grace.
- You get smaller and Christ gets bigger. This produces a godly self-forgetfulness quite different from self-loathing.
- You look at Christ, not just your sin.
- You get new energy, joy, gratitude, hope, perseverance, and purpose.

In lesson 9, we saw that Christ's life and death on our behalf makes us new creatures and defeats sin's power in our lives. In this lesson we have seen what it looks like to depend on the CROSS to deal with ongoing sin. We move ahead in the Christian life when we remember our new identity as regenerated, justified, and adopted sons and daughters. This new identity enables us to pursue the things that please God, as well as admit and turn from sin. It is a powerful dynamic that brings amazing freedom to the believer! We have a new identity and new power to change and fight the ongoing battle with sin.

# CPR

**Central Point**

1. CROSS-centered lives that transform us into the likeness of Christ are characterized by repentance and faith, which look deeply at sin as well as the grace of Christ.
2. Deep repentance is the fruit of a continual reliance on Christ's work on the CROSS for us.
3. Lasting change occurs when our heart's idols are unmasked and rejected, as we rely instead on Christ.

**Personal Application**

1. To live a CROSS-centered life, I need to exercise a repentance and faith that sees the depth of my waywardness and the power and glory of my Redeemer.
2. To change, I need to rely on my new legal status before God, which is mine because of what Christ has already done for me.
3. As I turn from my idols and turn to Christ, I can enjoy the freedom of faith and repentance in a new lifestyle that is pleasing to God.

**Relational Application**

1. Helping others live CROSS-centered lives involves helping them to see their ruling idolatries alongside the superiority of Christ.
2. To help others grow in holiness, I must link a clear call to repentance and faith to their new identity in Christ.
3. Biblical ministry calls me to help others unmask their idols (repentance) and encourage them to experience the joys of Christ's work in their behalf (faith).

## MAKE IT REAL

1. Horatius Bonar (1808–89) was known as the "prince of Scottish hymn-writers." He was also a pastor. He is quoted as saying,

> "No gloomy uncertainty as to God's favor can subdue one lust, or correct our crookedness of will. But the free pardon of the cross uproots sin, and withers all its branches. Only the certainty of love, forgiving love, can do this. Free and warm reception into

the divine favor is the strongest of all motives in leading a man to seek conformity to Him who has thus freely forgiven him all trespasses. A cold admission into the paternal house by the father might have repelled the prodigal, and sent him back to his lusts; but the fervent kiss, the dear embrace, the best robe, the ring, the shoes, the fatted calf, the festal song—all without one moment's suspense or delay, as well as without one upbraiding word, could not but awaken shame for the past, and true-hearted resolution to walk worthy of such a father, and of such a generous pardon. 'Revellings, banquetings, and abominable idolatries' come to be the abhorrence of him round whom the holy arms of renewed fatherhood have been so lovingly thrown. Sensuality, luxury, and the gaieties of the flesh have lost their relish to one who has tasted the fruit of the tree of life."

Reflect on the lesson in light of this quote as you continue to work on your Personal Growth Project. Ask yourself if you are maintaining a biblical emphasis on both Christ *for* you (justification and adoption) and *in* you (regeneration/sanctification). In what direction do you typically err?

2. With your Personal Growth Project before you, and in light of your typical ruling idolatries, what specifically about Christ do you need to see and believe as you engage in faith and repentance? What about Christ is more attractive than what you have settled for? What about Christ do you need to worship and adore? Be specific.

3. In light of your answers to questions 1 and 2, what passages of Scripture will help you see what you need to see about Christ? Avoid picking single verses. Instead, choose larger portions of Scripture that address both what you need to see about Christ and what new behavior should follow.

4. Using one of the Bible passages from this lesson, write out a prayer asking the Spirit to help you apply what you have learned to your life and relationships.

# FRUIT 1: Real Heart Change

## REVIEW/DISCUSS HOMEWORK (30 mins.)

Share with your small group how you are able to relate to Joe in the illustration from lesson 10. Share your answers to Make It Real questions 1–3.

Read together Review, CPR, and the Big Question.

## REVIEW

Now that we have covered ten of the twelve lessons, let's take some time to look at the Big Picture by stating the central point of each lesson covered so far.

- *Lesson 1*: Living with God's ultimate destination in view gives hope and perspective in our daily situations and relationships.
- *Lesson 2*: The hope of personal growth and change rests on my relationship with a person, Jesus Christ, who powerfully acts to change my heart and make it more and more like his.
- *Lesson 3*: God's work of personal transformation is intended to take place within the community of God's people.
- *Lesson 4*: Practical hope, comfort, and direction result from looking at our lives and our world from God's "big picture" perspective.
- *Lesson 5*: God understands the full range of joys and sorrows that make up our lives.
- *Lesson 6*: The Bible describes life this way: We live in a broken world as people who struggle daily.

- *Lesson 7*: The biblical picture of the THORN bush captures how sinners tend to respond sinfully to the blessings and difficulties of life.
- *Lesson 8*: All ungodly behavior grows out of a heart that has been captured by something other than Christ.
- *Lesson 9*: Because Christ now lives in me, I have everything I need to respond in new ways to what I face daily.
- *Lesson 10*: Living CROSS-centered lives that transform us into the likeness of Christ is the result of repentance and faith that looks deeply at sin alongside the magnificent grace of Christ.

This summary reminds us that the gloomy picture of sin and its destruction is overwhelmed by the love of God for his people. Good FRUIT in our lives is absolutely possible, even in difficult circumstances. Living God-centered, Christ-dependent lives that display the power and beauty of God is not just a possibility reserved for the uniquely godly, it is what any believer can experience when he relies on Christ. In this lesson, we will focus on good FRUIT with an eye toward the kind of heart that produces it. In lesson 12, we will see what good FRUIT itself looks like.

## CENTRAL POINT AND APPLICATION

*Central Point:* God's primary concern is obedience from the heart, not outward conformity to his law.

*Personal Application:* I need to pay attention to the issues of my heart as I seek to live in a godly way.

*Relational Application:* As I seek to help others, I want to celebrate good FRUIT in their lives even as I help them examine the beliefs that drive their good behavior.

# THE BIG QUESTION
### What type of heart produces good fruit?

# LESSON CONTENT

**DVD** (30 mins.)

**Small Group Activity** (30 mins.)

1. Read Deuteronomy 6:4–6 and Mark 12:28–31
    a. What do you think it means for God's commandments to be "on your heart"?

    *Possible answers include to have his word memorized, to live in obedience as an automatic response, to obey God with a right attitude—as a response to who God is.*

    b. What is the connection between the heart and obedience to God's commandments?

    *These passages show that the heart is central to obedience—anything less than heart obedience is empty and hypocritical.*

2. Read Jeremiah 31:31–34 and Ezekiel 36:24–28
    a. How do you see a connection between the heart and obedience in these passages?

    *Again God is promising to create a new covenant and will write it on their hearts so they do not go astray; in Ezekiel the "new heart" and Spirit will "move you to follow my decrees and ... keep my laws."*

    b. How do you see a connection between our hearts and our relationship with God?

    *God desires hearts that are pure and obedient to him; although God loves us and forgives us, he is not satisfied to allow us impure, idolatrous, or hard hearts.*

3. Read 1 Samuel 16:1–13
    a. What are some outward appearances that man tends to look at to determine quality?

    *Some possible answers include physical appearance, wealth, reputation, social ability, intellect, and occupation.*

b.  What are some qualities of the heart that God would deem desirable?

*Some possible answers include humility, selflessness, gentleness, other fruits of the Spirit, generosity, and compassion.*

4.  Read Psalm 139:23–24 and Psalm 86:11
    a.  How do you imagine God searching and testing someone's heart?

    *God already knows our hearts so the purpose of him searching and testing is really to reveal the results to you; God then searches and tests our hearts by bringing difficulty and opportunities to bear the fruit of the Spirit.*

    b.  What would be good about having God search and test your heart?

    *We experience God's grace; we grow in faith and knowledge; we become more like the image of Christ; we gain the opportunity to please him and glorify him.*

    c.  What do you think is meant by an "undivided heart"?

    *An undivided heart is one that does not doubt and waver; it is a heart that is fully devoted to seeking God.*

5.  Read Ephesians 3:14–21
    a.  According to this passage, where does the power to live the Christian life come from?

    *Our power comes through his Spirit which is within us (v. 16), "according to his power that is at work within us" (v. 20).*

# HOMEWORK

## "Out of the Overflow of the Heart"

The Bible uses the word *heart* to capture who we are at our core. The Hebrew and Greek words that are translated "heart" are used in several places to talk about being at the center of something (Deuteronomy 4:11—God is at the center of his people; Jonah 2:3—Jonah is in the center of the waves; Matthew 12:40—Jesus is buried deep in the earth). So it is significant that when the Bible talks about the Christian life, it talks about loving God with all of our *hearts*. God is not content living on the periphery of our lives. He will settle for nothing less than being at the center! Wholehearted devotion and joy is what God desires from us.

Contrast this to popular views of the Christian life. For most non-Christians (as well as many Christians), the Christian life is a matter of "keeping the rules." And while God *is* concerned with a person's behavior, the Bible offers a much fuller picture of a believer's life. It describes the Christian life in terms of a new and glorious relationship with God that brims with optimism and integrity and flows from the very core of our being! This new relationship was described in lesson 2, where we talked about our union with Christ. Everything we have and are is connected to who we are in Christ.

A Christian is someone whose life has been wonderfully invaded by the holy love of God. The response God seeks to create in us is nothing less than the pure, genuine love of our hearts. This is why God uses the metaphor of marriage to describe our relationship with him. This most intimate of human relationships only begins to describe the kind of relationship he is committed to having with us. The metaphor of marriage provides a richer context for understanding the importance of obeying God's commands and living a life of holiness.

## Illustration

Think of it this way. Suppose a single woman works in a large company with many employees. At one end of the office complex is a door with a bulletin board outside it. This is her boss's office; the bulletin board is where he posts the directions and rules for his employees. Let's say that she has just started working at this office and has never met the boss. What might she think of him and his bulletin board? Most likely, she would have a sense of awe and possibly some fear about the boss. The rules on the board could, therefore, be looked upon with a similar fear, and possibly distaste. The rules that are intended to regulate her behavior and maximize her office performance would not be particularly inspiring or motivating to her. Rather, they would be duties she believes she must carry out to avoid being fired.

Now imagine that, months later, the boss (who—conveniently for the sake of this illustration!—is a single man) develops an appropriate relationship with his employee and they begin to spend time with each other at church, with friends, and in many different contexts. Eventually they marry. Over that period of time, she notices that her perspective on the bulletin board has changed to the same degree that her heart is changing toward her new husband. She now sees the bulletin board instructions as wise and loving directions from someone who cares for her well-being. They are no longer viewed as burdensome but as specific ways she can honor and please her husband.

What has changed? Not the rules, but the nature of the relationship and the attitude of her heart toward the person who gave them. In some measure, this is the way the Bible talks about the Christian life. A new lifestyle—the outward FRUIT of a believer's life—does not grow out of a stoic obedience to the commands of God but from a heart that has been captured and captivated by the Giver of those commands.

My life is not determined by my upbringing, physiology, culture, emotions, or anything else. Because God has done everything necessary to meet my most basic need—redemption—I can be confident that change is absolutely possible for me. My biggest problem—sin—has been solved! God has redeemed me and given me a new heart—and thus the ability to live a new kind of life.

In light of the passages studied in this lesson, we look now at a person who allowed these truths to fully function in his life—the apostle Paul. To appreciate what we will see, we need to understand his circumstances. Remember that we have been stressing that good FRUIT is not just a remote possibility for the believer but something the Bible assumes can be present in our lives even in the most difficult circumstances.

Acts 16 tells us that Paul and Silas planted the church in Philippi. While there, they were thrown in prison for healing a slave girl. Paul later wrote Philippians while he was in a Roman prison for his faith. He wrote to encourage the Christians at Philippi to have joy in difficult circumstances.

### Instructions for Your Study of Philippians

**Leader,** a guide is provided as appendix 2, to give a few examples of the kinds of answers that would be appropriate. You may want to review it before you discuss this item together during the next session.

Read the questions below and then read the book of Philippians two or three times with them in mind. Next, answer each question using the truths found in the various verses. Put the answers in your own words. Focus especially on questions 5–7.

**?** 1. What is Paul's situation? (HEAT) What are his burdens, pressures, hardships, pains, and temptations, both actual and potential?

**?** 2. What responses might you expect to see in people who are in difficult circumstances? (THORNS) Think about how you and others typically react to the kinds of pressures Paul was under. What would be your thoughts, words, attitudes, emotions, and actions? Think also about how people typically react when things are going well. What temptations do blessings present?

**?** 3. What cravings and beliefs tend to rule the human heart, producing ungodly reactions? (THORNS) What false masters can rule in similar situations? What do verses like Philippians 1:17, 28; 2:3, 21; 3:3–7, 19; 4:6, 12; Acts 16:16, 19, 27 say about what those false masters might be?

**?** 4. What consequences follow sinful reactions? (THORNS) What vicious circles threaten the Philippians? That is, how would bad reactions compound hardship, create new problems, or spoil blessings? What do you reap when you react sinfully?

5. *What changes lives, inside and out? What rules the heart and produces godly responses? (CROSS) What specifically does God reveal about himself in Philippians? (Who is he? What is he like? What has he done? What is he doing? What will he do?) While you won't find everything there is to know about God in Philippians, what things stand out? More specifically, what captures Paul's attention when he looks at Christ? What rules Paul? How is Paul's life determined by faith? Why does Paul respond in such "unnatural" ways? What controls his interpretation of (and response to) his circumstances? What is the "secret" of contentment, peace, thankfulness, and joy? In what did Paul believe, trust, fear, hope, love, seek, and obey? How does faith in the Redeemer make the whole world look different? How does faith change us in practical ways? How do thankfulness, peacemaking, and contentment flow directly from believing, trusting, and fearing God?*

**?** 6. What specific good fruit do you observe? (FRUIT) How does Paul respond and what does he call all believers to do? How does Paul respond to negative and positive circumstances? What are concrete ways you are told to obey God?

**?** 7. What good effects result from the way Paul handled his situation? (FRUIT) That is, what positive, gracious outcomes does his faithful obedience create? How do these influence others around him? What positive consequences do you see or envision in your life? What challenges still remain? What new tensions will arise?

As you can see, the Bible shows us someone responding to trying circumstances in unique, surprising, and godly ways. This kind of behavior springs from a heart that is drinking in the resources of the gospel. They are readily available but must be drawn on by faith. Paul's life shows us that the Christian life is so much richer than merely obeying the rules! It is life lived in dependence upon and in relationship with the living Christ.

# CPR

## Central Point

1. God's primary concern is obedience from the heart, not just outward conformity to his law.
2. The hope and promise of the work of Jesus Christ addresses my greatest need—heart change.
3. God's love is demonstrated in the fact that he will not rest until he rules our hearts unchallenged.

## Personal Application

1. I need to pay attention to the issues of my heart as I seek to live in godly ways.
2. Being committed to heart change means being committed to an ongoing examination of the thoughts and desires of my heart.
3. I can live joyfully aware that Christ meets my greatest need—heart change.

## Relational Application

1. As I seek to help others, I need to celebrate the good FRUIT in their lives at the same time that I help them examine the beliefs that drive their good behavior.
2. I want to look for opportunities to help others examine the thoughts and desires of their hearts.
3. I am called to help others seek the only true help for their heart struggles, Christ.

# MAKE IT REAL

1. Has your Christian life been characterized by external obedience and minimal focus on your heart and your relationship with God? Examine all that you do. Are your activities motivated by a loving, grateful heart?

2. How are you responding to life's circumstances? Where do you see good FRUIT in your life? In what relationships do you see the good FRUIT of a life of faith? Where have you been patient with someone who tempts you to anger? Where have you lovingly confronted someone who makes you fearful? What recent difficulty has tested you and proven your faith genuine? What recent blessing has tested you and proven your faith genuine? Choose one of these questions and reflect on the kind of heart that produced the FRUIT. In what way did you intelligently rest in and rely on your Redeemer? What specific things were you repenting of (putting off) and believing in (putting on) that strengthened you to act courageously before God and others?

3. In light of the Philippians Bible Study, take the area of struggle you have chosen for your Personal Growth Project and ask yourself, "What are the things that rule my heart and therefore shape my behavior?"

- In what concrete ways do you need to embrace the promise of a new heart? How does God want to renew your heart in this area of struggle?

- How would believing, trusting, and embracing Christ change your actions, reactions, and responses?

- What new thoughts and desires in your heart would lead to a new harvest of good FRUIT responses?

- If hope, love, contentment, grace, forgiveness, self-control, peace, kindness, gentleness, patience, compassion, humility, and forbearance ruled your heart in this area of struggle, what new behavioral FRUIT would result?

Take time to meditate and pray over each answer, asking God to reveal your heart and change it. Embrace the opportunity this assignment gives you to experience the beginnings of the lasting heart change promised to you in Christ.

# FRUIT 2: New and Surprising Fruit

**Leader,** studying Paul's letter to the Philippians is a way to understand the biblical model of change as well as a means of self-examination and personal growth. Do not rush through your discussion of this study. Take time to reflect on the questions, allowing participants to share what they learned about their own heart struggles.

## REVIEW/DISCUSS HOMEWORK (30 mins.)

As a large group, discuss the Philippians Bible study.

In your small groups, share about how you evaluated your Christian life (question 1); share your answers to the Make It Real questions.

Read the Review, CPR, and the Big Question together.

In the last lesson we considered one of the most amazing, hope-filled promises of the new covenant—a new heart. God, the Giver of new hearts, is also the Savior who is constantly renewing them. In earlier lessons, we looked at how the sinful, THORN bush responses of thought, word, and deed have their roots in the THORN bush desires and motives of our hearts. In this lesson we will examine the grace-filled counterpart: how the heart change Christ brings leads to change in the way we respond—again, in thought, word, and deed—to the HEAT we encounter in the situations and relationships of this fallen world. This is the hope we find in Christ: in the scorching HEAT of trials, temptations, abundance, and want, God produces good FRUIT in us when we submit our hearts to him. We may prefer to be removed from the HEAT, but God often chooses to change us in the midst of it. How does this change take place? His grace changes the thoughts and motives of our hearts, as we saw in the last lesson. And as our hearts change, our outward lives—thoughts, words, and actions—change too.

## Central Point and Application

*Central Point:* Every Christian has the living water of the Holy Spirit flowing within and is already a fruit tree growing amid the heat of life's circumstances.

*Personal Application:* The fruit tree responses God calls me to are not impossible goals, but the result of the Spirit's work in me as a child of God.

*Relational Application:* I must help others to look at themselves with hope because the living water of Christ's Spirit flows within them.

# THE BIG QUESTION

Where is God calling you to embrace your potential as his child, and to be committed to the growth of new fruit that only his grace can produce? As you respond in new ways, how will your situations and relationships be changed?

## Lesson Content

**Leader,** if you are not using the DVD, and this will be your last session, you may want to consider reading this last lesson together. Please note that two DVDs are shown this session: Session 12 and the Conclusion.

**DVD** (24 mins.)

**Small Group Activity** (30–40 mins.)

Bible Passages
1. Read Isaiah 58
   a. How do we see that these people were obedient according to the law but not from their hearts? Their deeds and words seemed right, but their hearts were really cold.

      *Verses 2–3 show how they attempted to look good in their deeds, but vv. 3–7 show how their hearts were not sincere.*

b. Which verse shows the prospect of FRUIT if they turned their hearts truly toward God?

*The answer is verse 11: "you will be like a well-watered garden"—see also Jeremiah 31:12.*

2. Read Isaiah 55:1–2
   a. According to this passage, where does true satisfaction and delight come from?

   *from coming to God*

   b. What must we do to gain this true FRUIT? (What command verbs are present in this passage?)

   *We need to "come," "buy," and "listen."*

3. Read Hosea 14:5–7
   a. Apply the HEAT-THORNS-CROSS-FRUIT model to this passage.

   *HEAT = threat of Assyria. THORNS = they depended on man-made gods; they followed their own desires. CROSS = God's forgiveness, love them, show mercy. FRUIT = vv. 5–8.*

## DVD, Conclusion (16 mins.)

Go through the Make It Real questions at the end of this lesson, and discuss your answers together.

## HOMEWORK

Does the Bible shock you? It should! It is shocking in its honesty about the realities of life in this broken world. We see poverty, injustice, enslavement to sin, violence, failed governments, broken friendships and families, and a creation in decay. The Bible even addresses the difficulty of wisely handling abundance and ease! The Bible is also shocking in its hope, presenting us with a picture of possibility and potential far beyond anything we would expect. The Bible presents God's children as FRUIT-laden trees fed by endless streams of living water

(Isaiah 55:1–2; 58:11; Jeremiah 31:12; Hosea 14:5–7). Again and again when we expect parched earth and withered plants, the Bible presents an oasis of grace in the midst of the desert.

This lesson will examine the changes that take place in our actions and reactions when Christ changes our hearts by his grace. It may challenge some of your assumptions! For example:

1. Even after all we have learned, some of us still are tempted to say, "Because of what I have experienced, good things are not possible for me."
2. Others might still say, "God's 'rules' may work for others but not for me. I have tried to keep them during this trial, but it has not produced FRUIT in my life, only more frustration."
3. When we assume such things for ourselves, we tend to assume them for others too. We don't believe good FRUIT can grow in the HEAT of difficulty, so we give up on one another.

Let's consider how God's work of heart change helps us deal with the HEAT of life in new ways.

## Psalm 4

### In the Cave and Okay

Consider the following situation, and ask yourself what kind of person you would expect to find. This person is a highly respected leader with great power and influence over thousands of people. Yet within his own home he is powerless. He comes to realize that something is very wrong with his son. It is not just that his son is rebellious; he discovers that his son is doing all he can to destroy him and usurp his position. The man comes to the devastating realization that his son has turned many once-loyal subordinates against him. It is bad enough that he may lose his power and position, but it is crushing to think that his own son is the instigator. Then, just when he thinks that things are as bad as they can be, he learns that his son is planning to kill him! In his deep grief, he knows that he cannot fight for his position and kill his own son, so he flees home and goes into hiding.

Put yourself in this father's position. Imagine the depth of his grief and pain. Wouldn't you expect to find a bitter, angry father, rattling off a list of all the good things he did for his ungrateful son, and all the good things he taught him? Wouldn't you expect him to question God, especially since he had sought to be faithful to him? Can't you envision a man who reacts angrily to those around him? We would expect this father to be hopeless, cynical, and jaded regarding the spiritual counsel others might offer him.

Actually, we don't have to imagine this situation. It is recorded for us in 2 Samuel 14–18. The father was King David, and the son was Absalom! And yet, in David, we find something far different from what we would expect. Psalm 4 gives us a window into David's heart and life in the midst of his family tragedy.

Psalms 3 and 4 were written as morning and evening psalms when David was hiding in a cave with a band of faithful followers, fleeing from Absalom. They help us to understand his heart and behavior. When you know the story behind Psalm 4, you cannot help but be impressed by what you find there. David is in one of the most painful experiences of his life, and what do we see him doing?

1. *He does not run away from God.* He does not question God's faithfulness or bitterly rehearse how the promises and principles of Scripture have failed. David places himself, again, in God's hands. He turns *toward* God, pleading for him to hear and do what only he can do (vv. 1–2).

2. *He reminds himself of his identity as God's child.* Your sense of who you are powerfully shapes your response to life. David tells himself, "I must remember that I am one of God's '*set apart ones.*' And since I have been set apart by God, I can be assured that when I cry, he will always hear me. I don't know why God put this difficulty in my life, but I know he hears me as I cry out in the midst of it" (v. 3).

3. *He examines his own heart.* David does something very different from our normal instincts in times of trial. He does not look outside himself, endlessly rehearsing how bad his circumstances are and how evil his son is, growing more and more discouraged and bitter. No, he looks inside himself (v. 5) to examine his own heart. In trial, our hearts are attacked and revealed. We need to know and guard our hearts because what we do in moments of difficulty is not forced on us by the situation, but by how we think and what we desire in the middle of it.

4. *He worships.* That is what the words in verse 5 mean. Often, when we are in pain and difficulty, we are tempted to skip our personal devotions and be inconsistent in attending corporate worship. We allow ourselves to miss small group meetings and decide not to get involved in ministry opportunities. In so doing, we withhold from God the sacrifices of our worship and service. But when you peek into the cave of Psalm 4, we don't find David complaining—we find him worshipping!

5. *He ministers.* David was not in the cave alone; he had been followed by a band of the faithful. But as David worshipped, these men began to panic (v. 6, "What good is ever going to come out of this mess?"). How does David respond to their fears? He doesn't impatiently say that they should know better; he doesn't ignore them and go off by himself. No, he ministers to them. He prays that they would clearly see God. In the midst of this most painful drama, David prays for those around him, asking God to shine the blessing of his presence on them so that they can rest.

6. *He rests (vv. 7–8).* We might expect sad and sleepless nights, and certainly, David was grieving. But here he talks of joy! He talks about sleeping in peace! Why isn't he overcome with fear, bitterness, anger, and dread? The answer is simple yet profound: *because his heart is controlled by something else.* His heart isn't ruled by the comfort and status of palace life. His heart is ruled by God and the reality that he is one of God's children. David hasn't lost the thing most precious to him. The safety, security, and stability of his life are not about location and situation but about his relationship to God. David still has what makes him happy and secure, so he can sleep even in crushing disappointment.

Are you tempted to respond, "This guy is just not real"? Actually, David's worst choices did not come amid difficulty but amid awesome blessing—another kind of temptation. When he was in an unchallenged position of power, he was not satisfied. He ended up stealing another man's wife and arranging his murder. David was a vulnerable sinner, just like us. There were times when he remembered who he was and lived on the basis of what he had been given as God's child. There were other times he did not. That is why this psalm holds out so much hope—it reflects God's work in sinful people just like you and me. FRUIT trees *do* grow in the harsh, hot sun—in the lives of real people in a broken world.

Don't read this passage and simply say, "This is what I *should* be doing, but I'm not!" Say, "This is what God is doing in me too. These things are possible for me, too, because David's Redeemer is my Redeemer. The God who ruled David's heart and gave him peace is in my heart as well. I can make good choices, do good things, and harvest good FRUIT, even amid the hardest challenges of life!"

Psalm 4 does not picture a man's mechanical obedience to a set of biblical principles. If all we needed was information on how to respond to tough situations, Jesus never would have needed to come. What we see in this psalm is the grace of God at work in a man's heart, empowering him to do things that would be impossible on his own. Christ's work on the CROSS makes that same grace available to you and me.

The point is, God does more than deliver us from the HEAT. He delivers us from *ourselves* so that we can stand up *under* the HEAT and not merely survive but bear good FRUIT. Under the pressure of family difficulty, love can grow. Under the HEAT of unappreciated sacrifice, perseverance can grow. In the middle of physical suffering, peace and sturdy faith can blossom. In the midst of want, giving can grow where the THORNS of greed and selfishness once lived. Under the HEAT of life in a fallen world, new and surprising FRUIT can and does grow.

## Galatians 5:13—6:10

Streams in the Desert

In John 7:37–38, Jesus says that whoever believes in him will have "streams of living water flow from within him." John notes that Jesus was referring to the Holy Spirit. As he indwells us as the children of God, spiritual rivers of living water produce life where there was death. New FRUIT grows as our hearts are changed by the Spirit, even in the HEAT of life in our world.

Galatians 5:13—6:10 pictures the kind of FRUIT that grows because of the Spirit's presence and work. You may be thinking, *I understand that the Holy Spirit lives in me and that the Bible likens him to living water. But I am not sure what this means when I face the difficulty of trials and the temptations of blessings.* This passage explains what Christ meant in John 7.

The passage begins with a warning against self-indulgence (vv. 13–15). We all know that sin causes us to be more committed to ourselves than anything else. It causes us to love ourselves more than anyone else, to be more concerned about our own welfare than anything else. Sin makes us self-centered and self-indulgent as we give in to the desires of the sinful nature and feed its cravings. Such selfish living destroys relationships and harms people. Our chief problem in relationships is not the fallen world we live in, but the fact that we ourselves are deeply self-centered and have trouble loving one another.

Notice, however, that this passage does not end on a note of struggle. It pictures people who are committed to ministry in the face of others' sin, who look for ways to bear the burdens of others and do good (6:1–10). The passage begins with THORN bush responses and ends with FRUIT tree living! What makes the difference? The living water of the Holy Spirit! Christ who lives within every believer. He battles with our sinful nature on our behalf. Because of him, we do not need to yield to the sinful nature. Our union with Christ enables us to say no to motivating emotions (passions) and powerful cravings (desires) and go in the opposite direction (see v. 24).

As we say yes to the indwelling Holy Spirit, his living water produces new FRUIT in our hearts: love, joy, peace, patience, kindness, goodness, faithfulness, gentleness, and self-control. These character qualities aren't unrealistic standards that God holds over us; they are gifts of the Spirit produced *in* us. This change *within* us changes the way we respond to the things and the people *around* us (the HEAT). And this is the FRUIT that results: Kind people look for ways to do good even when circumstances are tough. Patient and faithful people don't run away when things are tough or people mess up. Loving people look for ways to minister even when they have been sinned against. Gentle people see a person struggling and look for ways to help him bear his burden.

Galatians 5 and 6 are filled with hope. We must reject a view of the Christian life that says that God calls us to the impossible. The true picture is that God meets us in the trials and challenges of life and he doesn't just give us rules—he gives us his Son, Jesus Christ! Because of him, what we are called to do is neither unrealistic nor impossible.

Look at the FRUIT tree carefully. Note that its FRUIT grows under the scorching HEAT of difficulty. Then remind yourself, "I *am* that tree as a child of God. Its FRUIT is God's gift, produced by his Spirit in me. I cannot be satisfied with THORN bush responses to life. I need not look at what God calls me to and be discouraged by its apparent impossibility. God calls me to be filled with hope and to believe that I am who he says I am—a tree bearing FRUIT in the middle of the desert."

## New and Surprising Fruit

In light of what we have learned about the cross (lessons 9 and 10) and how it transforms my heart (lesson 11), let's consider how his grace will be demonstrated in my life.

*1. I will live with personal integrity.* As God's grace transforms my heart, I no longer need to be afraid to look at myself in the mirror of God's Word. I no longer need to defend or excuse myself. I no longer need to rationalize my sinful choices or shift the blame to someone or something else. I no longer need to deny or avoid my sin. Why? Because if the God of forgiveness, wisdom, and power actually lives in me, why would I be afraid to face my weaknesses, failures, immaturity, or sin? Instead, I can be *committed to grow in self-understanding.* I can be glad that God's Word is a mirror into my heart. I can be glad that the people God puts in my life help me to see myself more accurately. I can be excited about my potential to see, learn, change, and grow.

I will also *seek godly help.* Again, God's grace not only frees me from my slavery to sin; it opens me up to the unending resources of God's grace. One of those resources is the Body of Christ. Think of it this way: If I am encouraged that the ultimate Helper lives within me, I will take advantage of all the resources he gives me in the body of Christ. I will not live independently or self-sufficiently. I will take advantage of all the biblical teaching available to me. I will seek the fellowship of a small group. I will ask to be shepherded by my elders. I will pursue the wisdom of mature brothers and sisters. I will try to benefit from the accountability a close friend can provide. And I will take advantage of these resources by being honest about my struggles of heart and behavior.

As I do all of this, I will *express godly emotions.* There is no scene more emotional than the scene on Calvary. On the cross, Christ cried out to his Father as he suffered and died. The grace of the cross invites you to cry out to the Father as well. Christ cried to a Father who was silent as he let him die so that you could cry to a Father who will hear you and give you what you need to live.

The more you understand who God is and who he has made you to be, the more you realize that the Christian life is not an emotionless, stoic existence. On earth, Christ expressed a whole range of emotions, and, as you grow in Christ, you will too. Maturity is about the right emotion expressed in the right way at the right time. As Christians, we should be the saddest (because we understand the ravages of sin) and the most joyful (because we experience the grace of Christ) people on earth.

There is a proper time for sorrow, joy, anger, fear, sadness, jealousy, happiness, gratitude, dread, anticipation, remorse, grief, and excitement. The life of faith is a stained-glass window, rich with the color of many different emotions, through which the light of Christ shines.

*2. I will let grace shape my relationships.* As people who have had God's grace poured out on our lives, it only makes sense for us to share that grace with others. Jesus told a story illustrating this principle in Matthew 18:21–35. Because the people around you are (like you) still sinners, they will fail, they will sin against you, and they will disappoint you. That is when you can extend to them the same grace you have received. Our anger, irritation, impatience, condemnation, bitterness, and vengeance will never produce good things in their lives. But God *can* produce good things in them when we are willing to incarnate his grace. When we do, we become part of what he is doing in their lives, instead of standing in the way. So, what does it mean practically to let that grace shape your relationships?

It means *being ready, willing, and able to forgive* (Matthew 6:12–15; Mark 11:25). The decision to forgive is first a heart transaction between you and God. It is a willingness to give up your desire to hold onto (and in some way punish the person for) his offense against you. Instead, you entrust this person and the offense to God, believing that he is righteous and just. You make a decision to respond to this person with grace and forgiveness. This vertical transaction (between you and God) prepares you for the horizontal transaction of forgiveness between you and the offending person, when you are given that opportunity.

Let's face it: we are sinners living with sinners, so there is never a day when forgiveness isn't needed. The refusal to forgive, the temptation to replay an offense in our minds, and our thoughts of punishment and revenge all damage the relationships God wants to use to make us more like him. They are workrooms for his grace in our lives. In this important area of forgiveness, (1) the grace of God causes me to want others to know the same forgiveness Christ purchased for me, and (2) it changes me, enabling me to genuinely forgive others.

It means *humbly asking for forgiveness.* When I ask for forgiveness, I admit my responsibility for a sin against you, without any justification, excuse, or blame. Here is what it sounds like: "I was wrong for _____. Please forgive me. I am sorry for the pain I caused you."

The three parts of this request define what seeking forgiveness is all about. First, seeking forgiveness means coming to someone I have wronged with an attitude of humble honesty. ("I was wrong for _____.") Second, seeking forgiveness acknowledges that I have sinned against the other person, and I therefore need to ask him to be part of the forgiveness process as well. ("Please forgive me.") It is not enough to say you are sorry. When we do this, we deny people the blessing of actually granting us forgiveness. Third, a request for forgiveness always should include a compassionate acknowledgment of the pain my sin caused. ("I am sorry for the pain I caused you.") Here again, I am experiencing the results of God's grace. His grace reminds me that I am a sinner—if I weren't, there would be no need for Christ's death. But his grace does more: it changes my heart, making me sensitive to the sin I was once blind to and ready to admit what I once would have excused.

When the grace of God shapes my relationships, I *respond to the sin and weakness of others with grace.* Do you hold people to higher standards than you hold yourself? Do you tend to forget that you are a sinner, while remembering that others are? Do you fail to overlook minor offenses? Do you spend more time catching people doing wrong than doing right? Are you better at criticizing than encouraging? Do people feel accepted and loved by you or criticized and judged? How do you tend to respond to the weaknesses, sins, and failures of those around you?

Grace enables me to serve others out of a heart of compassion, gentleness, forbearance, kindness, patience, and love. The closer I get to people, the more these attitudes are needed because that is when I begin to be affected by their weaknesses and sin (and vice versa). The closer we are to one another, the more our hearts are revealed. Thus we all need to ask is, "What attitudes shape my closest relationships?" Christ lives in us to rescue us from ourselves, so that we can be loving and gracious with one another even though we are sinners. Each time I lay aside my own desires, to serve another, I am living out the results of Christ's death on the cross.

*3. God's grace gives purpose and direction to my words and actions.* God calls his children to actions that reflect the grace we have received in Christ. The question is, "Does this grace shape my relationships?" Let's look at some of the grace-based actions to which Christ calls us, actions that are part of the new FRUIT of faith in our lives.

- Grace enables each of God's children to *make peace* (James 3:13–18). Where, right now, do you need to be committed to peace?

- Grace enables each of God's children to *speak the truth* (Ephesians 4:25). Where, right now, can problems be solved, relationships restored, and people blessed by your clear speaking of truth?
- Grace enables each of God's children to *serve others* (Galatians 5:14–15). Where, right now, is God calling you to be a servant?
- Grace enables each of God's children to *grant forgiveness* to those who seek it (Luke 17:1–10). If I have given the offense up to God and refuse to be vengeful, my heart is ready to grant forgiveness when the offender seeks me out. The vertical transaction with God when I let go of the offense prepares me for the horizontal transaction with the person who sinned against me.
- Grace enables each of God's children to *learn to say no*. That response is not because we fail to love others, but because we are committed to do what is right because we love them *and* God. In the Gospels, Jesus did not do everything others wanted him to do. He was instead motivated by his Father's will. (See fig. 12-1, an illustration/study from the Gospel of John.) Christian love does not make us slaves to the agenda of others; it makes us slaves and servants of Christ, and therefore willing to serve others. There will be times when my allegiance to Christ means that it is loving and right to say no to other people's requests.
- Grace enables each of God's children to *recognize, develop, and use the gifts* he has given for his glory and the good of others (See Romans 12:1–8). What are your God-given gifts? How should they be used where God has placed you?

"Christ-in-me" living gives a purpose and direction to all my actions and words. No longer motivated by my own agenda, I now want my life to reflect what God is doing in me. I want my life to be part of what he is doing in others' lives, here and around the world. This results in surprising new FRUIT in my actions, choices, and words. Where once I made war, I now make peace. Where once I tried to get others to serve me, I now look for ways to serve them. Where once I was ruled by fear of others and said yes way too often, I now am motivated by God's practical will and understand when I must say no. Where once I used my God-given gifts for my own benefit and glory, I now use them for God's glory and the benefit of others. Where I once trimmed and twisted the truth to get what I wanted, I now lovingly speak the truth, even when it may be costly. Where once I held on to bitterness and anger, I now give the offense to the Lord and extend forgiveness to others.

As I examine such new FRUIT in my life, what do I say? "Wow, what a good person I am"? No, I humbly and joyfully affirm that these things are in my life because "it is no longer I who lives, but Christ lives in me." The harvest of good consequences that result are a hymn to the presence, grace, love, wisdom, and power of my crucified and risen Redeemer.

**Leader,** a guide is provided as appendix 3, to give a few examples of the kinds of answers that would be appropriate. You may want to review it before you discuss.

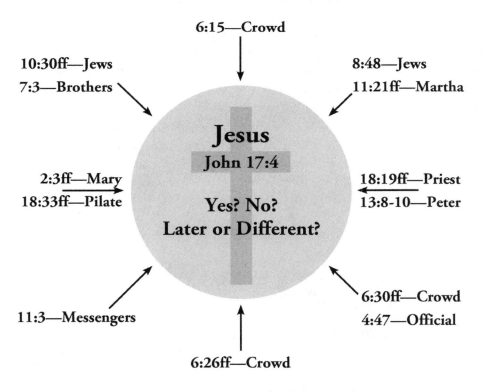

*Figure 12-1.* Learning to Say No (Christ, Our Example)

## What If I Fail?

There is probably never a day when we do not fail at doing what Christ, on the cross, has enabled us to do. Yes, God's grace has changed us. It gives us power over what once enslaved us. It has opened our blind eyes, softened our hard hearts, and given wisdom to our foolish minds. Yet, with all of these wonderful gifts flowing from our union with Christ, sin still remains in us. That's the *reason* you need to know that the cross has broken the power of sin—because the presence of sin still remains! We should not be shocked that the war still goes on inside us. We have been changed, we have been empowered, but we have not yet been perfected.

So what do you do when you fail? Do you excuse and rationalize? Do you wallow in self-defeating guilt and regret? God's grace calls you away from both responses and gives you the freedom to admit your sin and repent. It is impossible for your sin to shock the One who died because of it. His grace also gives you the freedom to seek and receive forgiveness each time you fall. We do not have to carry the sins Christ took on himself. He paid the price we could not pay so that we would never have to pay it again.

When you fail, keep his forgiving grace in view. Run *to* your Lord, not away from him. Receive his forgiveness, get back up, and follow him once more, knowing that each time you fail, you can experience the glories of your identity as one for whom Christ died. Each failure reminds us of why he had to die; each confession reminds us of the amazing forgiveness that only the cross could provide.

## Putting It All Together

What are some practical implications of the fact that FRUIT trees grow in the harsh HEAT of life?

1. You are already that FRUIT tree because of what Christ has done. There are already evidences of godly character and strengths in your life. By faith, recognize the good FRUIT that results from responding to the gospel and the Spirit's work in your life.

2. The Christian life is about living by faith in Christ, with the sense of possibility, privilege, and appreciation he brings. It is not about grudgingly "keeping the rules" as an angry, bitter person in a "grin-and-bear-it" lifestyle.

3. Because Christ has made me a new creature, good things are possible even under great HEAT. His work in my heart enables me

to respond in ways that produce good FRUIT, even when bad things are happening.

4. These good things are possible because I have been united with Christ and indwelt by his Spirit. Trial and temptation do not negate the reality of hope. Rather, they are opportunities to experience the power of God at work.

5. God calls you to a new identity in Christ ("this is who I am") and therefore a new way of living ("this is what I can be"), all rooted in the active presence of Christ in my life. Change is not rooted in a body of knowledge, a set of rules and expectations, theological outlines, or behavioral techniques. Lasting biblical change is the result of our hearts' transformation by the grace of the risen Lord Jesus. Only as his grace rules our hearts can we have hope of keeping his commands and following the principles of his Word.

# CPR

## Central Point

1. Christ's work on the CROSS has made every believer a FRUIT tree that bears FRUIT in the HEAT of difficulty through the living water of the Spirit within.

2. The Bible clearly depicts people responding to difficulty in remarkable ways.

3. In times of struggle, God never calls me to do anything without providing the spiritual resources for me to do it.

## Personal Application

1. I must not look at the FRUIT tree responses God desires as impossible goals but as the results of the Spirit's work in me as a child of God.

2. Because of my union with Christ and the Spirit, I must always remember my FRUIT tree identity and potential.

3. God's primary goal is not to protect me or deliver me from difficulty but to change me in it and through it.

**Relational Application**

1. I must help others to see themselves with hope because of Christ's Spirit living within them.
2. The Bible does not present us with noble people who never fail but with a God of grace who has given us in Christ all we need to defeat sin and deal with difficulty.
3. I must help people to see that Christ is with them in temptation and difficulty, empowering them to stand strong and do what is right.

## MAKE IT REAL

Take a final look at yourself in light of what you have learned through this course and your Personal Growth Project. List the following:

- New things you have learned about life in a fallen world (HEAT).

- New things you have learned about your actions, reactions, and words (THORNS).

- New things you have learned about the thoughts, motives, treasures, idols, desires, and purposes of your heart (THORNS).

- New things you have learned about Christ's work, your identity as God's child, and Christ's heart-transforming grace (CROSS).

- New things you have learned about where God is calling you to grow and change (FRUIT).

- New things you have learned about the struggles of others and how God can use you in their lives (FRUIT).

- New ways you can be thankful for Christ and his ongoing work in your life (CROSS).

Write out a prayer of thanksgiving, listing those things which the Spirit has taught you in the last weeks.

# *How Being Married to Christ Should Change the Way We Respond to Life*

(Leader Guide to Discussion on pp. 41–42)

Leader, this discussion is intended to help participants understand the practical, daily benefits of our marriage to Christ. All of us respond to life based on who we think we are and what we think we have. The 4'5" teenager probably will give up his dream of being a basketball star. The uneducated man probably won't seek to be a college professor. Peter talks about Christians whose lives lack effectiveness and productivity because they have forgotten who they are and, because of this, have not pursued all that is theirs in Christ (2 Peter 1:3–9). This discussion is intended to show how our present union with Christ impacts our experiences in this fallen world. It is meant to help your group grasp how different their responses will be when they are rooted in the reality of their present union with Christ.

To help you lead the discussion, we have prepared several responses to the situations listed. Use this to shape your responses to other items on the list. Choose a few for group discussion, and do all you can to help participants develop their own responses to the other situations.

*1. Loss of a job.* In our culture, a well-paying job is an important thing. Yet it can go beyond being an *important* thing to being a source of personal security and identity. When this happens, the loss of a job not only brings financial stress, but it rocks one's sense of well-being at a profound level. People tend to define who they are by what they do.

They attach their identity to something they have no guarantee will be there tomorrow. Contrast this with approaching your career with a deep appreciation of your identity in Christ. When I live this way, the loss of a job will not mean the loss of identity or personal security. I will understand that the most valuable things in my life are not at stake when I lose my job. Because of my marriage to Christ, I am never alone in these dark moments. I understand that I have resources that go far beyond my personal wisdom, character, and strength to deal with the pain, loss, fear, and discouragement. I can rest in the fact that the One to whom I am married is not only in control of the details of my life but has my good as his goal. All this protects me from discouragement and enables me to respond with courage and faith to a difficult moment of life.

2. *Working at a job that is unending, exhausting, and thankless, with no prospect of advancement.* It is a human tendency to look outside ourselves to relationships, circumstances, and accomplishments for a sense of fulfillment. This makes it difficult to be stuck in an unsatisfying job with no way out. But when we live with an inner sense of fulfillment because of our relationship with Christ, we do not approach life feeling needy. Rather, we face each day with a contentment and joy that no job could ever give.

Imagine grasping the fact that we have been chosen from the mass of humanity to live in a present, intimate union with Christ. Every detail of our lives is carefully controlled; we have been called by God's grace, forgiven of every one of our sins, and indwelt by God himself (in the person of the Holy Spirit). It is amazing even to be *tolerated* by God. It would be an honor simply to be *invited* to the wedding. It is beyond our comprehension to be the beloved *bride* of the King of kings and the Lord of lords. When I begin to understand this, my heart comes to life with a sense of the honor, privilege, and blessing that is mine. It changes the way I think about the unfulfilling circumstances of my life. Yes, my job bores me. Yes, I had always hoped to do something more significant. Yes, I wish I could find a way out. But I am not depressed or discouraged because I do not go to work searching for fulfillment. In Christ I am joyful and satisfied. Although I have a thankless job, I know that Christ never forgets the things I do in his name. Although my job is boring, as the bride of Christ, I am connected to the most important things in the universe. My union with Christ gives meaning and purpose to everything I do and say.

*3. Your never-ending burden as a single parent.* It is hard not to panic when you realize that you have a job that was meant for two. It seems impossible and unfair. These reactions are often rooted in a crucial mistake: We look to *ourselves* to see if we have the wisdom and strength to do what needs to be done. When we realize that we don't, we get discouraged, angry, and bitter. We have forgotten who we are in Christ.

No single parent has the wisdom needed to care for his or her children, but Christ is the source of all wisdom and he promises to give it to his bride. No single parent has the strength needed for the job, but Christ's strength is made perfect when we are weak. No single parent has the godly character the role requires, but Christ has given us his Spirit so that we have the power to do and say what is right. When I approach single parenthood with an appreciation of my marriage to Christ, I am not discouraged or overwhelmed by an admittedly difficult role. I see my huge responsibilities, but I also see Christ and his full provision for me.

*4. Chronic sickness, injury, or disease.* We all tend to assume that we will always be as healthy or that, at worst, any physical pain we encounter will be temporary. In this way we subtly base our sense of well-being on our physical health. Physical suffering *is* hard, but it is made much harder if physical health has been our source of rest, security, and well-being. In a fallen world our bodies are always at risk and always wasting away, and thus not a safe thing on which to place our hope.

Imagine the difference it makes to believe that the most precious things in life are not physical, that although poor health can make your life difficult, it cannot rob you of your identity, your meaning and purpose, your joy, or your sense of personal rest. This is exactly what happens when you respond to physical suffering with your awareness of being eternally united to Christ. Paul says it this way: "Outwardly we are wasting away, yet inwardly we are being renewed day by day" (2 Corinthians 4:16). Because of our marriage to Christ, no matter what our physical condition, we are strengthened by new mercies every morning, daily encouraged by God's love, and empowered by the Spirit every moment. Yes, we would like to retain our strength, avoid chronic pain, and escape disease, but we don't assess our lives based on our physical condition. We fix our eyes on the glorious, unseen reality of our union with Christ and the resources that are ours because we are married to him.

Leader, these four examples show how an appreciation of our marriage to Christ alters the way we experience life's circumstances. The principle is the same in each one. We must evaluate our lives in terms of what is unseen. When we look at life through the lens of our marriage to Christ, we see that we have everything we need to deal with life. We get tired but not discouraged. We will be sad but not hopeless. We will endure pain, but we will not give up. We see that our lives do not consist in what we have, how we feel, or what we have accomplished, but in who we *are* in Christ. This enables us to stand where we would have once fallen down.

Help your group to understand the practical value of these truths. Help them to see that when you believe them and live on that basis, it makes a huge difference in your view of yourself and your response to life. Brainstorm about how these truths can practically impact their responses to life. Help them to make concrete connections between their behavior and this biblical truth.

# Philippians Bible Study

(Leader Guide to Questions on pp. 163–66)

**Leader,** as you use this, be open to a host of different answers. This is simply a guide.

*What is Paul's situation?*
> Acts 16/Philippians 1:12–14: Paul is in prison.
> 1:16–17: There are rivalries within the church.

*What responses might you expect to see in people in difficult circumstances?*
> Use your imagination or have your students describe what their temptations might be. Anger, frustration, despair, questioning God's goodness and wisdom, forsaking the faith, self-sufficiency, self-righteousness, and preoccupation with protecting your comfort are all possible responses. No doubt the possibilities for sin vary with every individual.

*What cravings and beliefs tend to rule the human heart, producing ungodly reactions?*
> 1:17; 2:3, 21; 3:19: selfish ambition
> 1:28; Acts 16:16, 19, 27: fear of man
> 3:1–7: self-righteousness

*What consequences follow sinful reactions?*
> 1:15–18: fighting between people
> 3:18–19: personal destruction and eternal punishment

*What changes lives, inside and out? What rules the heart and produces godly responses?*
> 1:2: grace and peace that are ours through Christ

1:6; 2:13: a faithful, sovereign God

1:19: the Holy Spirit of Christ

1:20–21: confidence in the resurrected Christ

2:1–11: seeing Christ's humble service in behalf of his people

2:1–8; 3:10–11: identifying with Christ's sufferings. If he suffered, why should I assume that I should not? Suffering should not be avoided. Suffering can be redemptive. It is proof of my union with Christ!

2:9–11, 16: trusting in the exalted Christ. If he was exalted, so shall I be one day! This world is not all there is.

3:1–9: resting in the all-sufficient, justifying work of Christ for you

3:12–14: seeing that Christ has taken hold of you and will not let go

3:20–21: the glorious return of Christ

1:1, 5, 14, 25; 2:19; 3:17; 4:10, 18: the example of others

1:9, 19: others' prayers

2:12–13: We change ourselves *as God enables us.*

4:4–7: true worship of the living God

4:8–9: meditating on the truth

*What specific good FRUIT do you observe? 1:3–11: love and prayer for others*

1:12–13, 15–18: a concern for Christ's reputation, not Paul's

1:3: thanksgiving!

1:6, 12, 19–26; 2:9–11; 3:13, 20–21: courage

2:1: encouragement, comfort, and fellowship with Christ and the Spirit

2:2–4: humility, tenderness, compassion for others

2:12–18: vigor to pursue holiness in the midst of difficulty

2:19–30: godly emotions of struggle rather than stoicism

4:11–12: contentment; not playing the part of the victim, even though Paul is being flagrantly sinned against

*What good effects result from the way Paul handled his situation?*

1:13: People are evangelized.

1:14: Other Christians are encouraged to be bold.

1:19: Other believers are encouraged to pray. Present-day readers have the same experience as we read this letter!*

---

* The Philippians Bible Study was formulated by CCEF faculty member David Powlison as part of CCEF's course, Dynamics of Biblical Change, and has been used by permission.

# *Helps for Figure 12-1*

## (Leader Guide to p. 183)

Although Jesus was a perfect picture of God's kindness and love on earth, he was willing to say no or "later" to requests, desires, agenda, or threats that would take him outside his Father's will. His focus on the mission he was sent to do gave him a way to filter the agenda of others. Though he was under all kinds of outside pressure, Jesus remained true to the work his Father had given him to do. Below are examples from the Gospel of John.

- *2:3–4:* Jesus is with his mother at the wedding in Cana. Mary encourages Jesus to provide more wine. Jesus tells her that he is not ready.
- *4:43–54:* A royal official pleads with Jesus to go to his sick son in Capernaum. Jesus refuses but says that the son will live. It is reported that the son's fever broke at the exact time Jesus said this to the father.
- *6:15:* The crowd, motivated by Jesus' ability to feed them miraculously, decides to take him by force and make him their king. He hides from them in the mountains because such an earthly kingdom is not in his Father's plan.
- *6:26–27:* When the crowd catches up with Jesus, he makes it clear that he will not become their king because they want his leadership for the wrong reason.
- *6:30–40:* Jesus refuses to perform a miracle to induce the crowd to believe and then confronts their unbelief.
- *7:3–10:* Jesus' brothers encourage him to leave Galilee to celebrate the Feast of Tabernacles in Judea. Jesus knows that the Jews

are waiting to kill him and that it is not yet his time to die, so he lets his brothers go and then goes alone, keeping his trip a secret.

- *8:48–59:* Jesus will not give in to what the Jews want him to confess (that he is a fraud) even though his life is at stake. He reaffirms his messiahship and flees as they prepare to kill him.
- *10:30–39:* Again, Jesus is unwilling to deny or dilute his messianic claims because of fear of the Jews. Instead, he confronts their unbelief and then flees. Notice the pattern. He is unwilling to fail in doing the Father's will by succumbing to the threats of the Jews, but he does not linger because it is not yet his time to die.
- *11:1–6:* Jesus refuses to go to Lazarus's sickbed despite the disciples' urging; he knows that Lazarus's death will give him an opportunity to demonstrate his power over life and death. Jesus intends to respond to this situation in a way that demonstrates his messiahship (vv. 14–15) even though his response will be misunderstood by his friends and ensure Lazarus's death.
- *11:21–27:* Jesus' schedule is different than Martha's. He knows the importance of Lazarus's resurrection to his messianic mission, so he stays away until Lazarus dies though that made no sense to Martha.
- *13:8–10:* Peter objects to his master washing his feet like a servant, but Jesus knows the importance of this act for Peter and all who would read of it. He does not relent at Peter's protest and uses the moment to teach important truths.
- *18:19–24:* Jesus refuses to soften his message before the High Priest though he understands the man's power and the suffering that speaking candidly will bring. Jesus is faithful to his mission even when threatened.
- *18:33–37:* Under threat of his life, Jesus is clear about his message. He came to earth to establish a kingdom that is not of this world. He testifies to these truths without succumbing to the agenda of the High Priest or Pilate.

# At a Glance: How People Change

④ Life as God Sees It, Change as God Does It

⑤ The Real God in the Real World

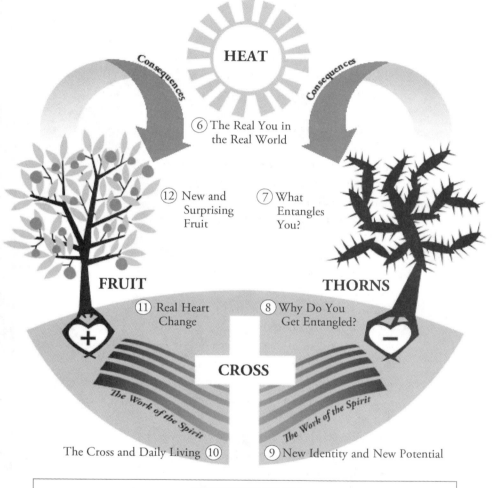

HEAT

Consequences     Consequences

⑥ The Real You in the Real World

⑫ New and Surprising Fruit     ⑦ What Entangles You?

FRUIT     THORNS

⑪ Real Heart Change     ⑧ Why Do You Get Entangled?

CROSS

The Work of the Spirit     The Work of the Spirit

The Cross and Daily Living ⑩     ⑨ New Identity and New Potential

---

**THE FOUNDATION**

① Here's Where God Is Taking You     ② So, You're Married to Christ

③ Change Is a Community Project